LISTEN TO THE LAND

LISTEN TO THE LAND

A Farm Journal Treasury
By the Editors of Farm Journal
Edited by Kathryn Larson

Countryside Press
a division of Farm Journal, Inc.
Philadelphia, Pennsylvania

Distributed to the trade by
PRENTICE-HALL, INC.
Englewood Cliffs, New Jersey

810.8
F

Book Design: Alfred Casciato

Photos: Charles Brill, 98, 226; Jean Gillies, 26; Grant Heilman, 10, 140, 162, 200; Bob Hirsch, 56; Perry L. Struse, 116; U.S. Department of Agriculture, 72, 176; Joan Liffring Zug, 248.

ISBN: 0-13-537084-1

Library of Congress Catalog Card Number 76-56946

Contents

A Good Life as Well as a Good Living

In our 200 years of nationhood, Americans have moved from farm to city in an accelerating migration toward "a better life," or at least toward opportunity as they perceived it.

Now, an ever-increasing number of the city's disillusioned are looking outward from their urban existence wondering where it is—this better life. Some, especially younger environmentalists, are moving back to the land, new pioneers in a world no longer simple (if it ever was). Others are eyeing it with yearning, feeling sure that a return to a "natural" environment will simplify their existence and bring happiness. Many are exploring it two weeks at a time, on farm vacations or camping trips. Or on Sundays they seek the peace of byways, driving past fields of grazing livestock and waving grain.

But what is it really like—living on the cows' side of the fence? The best way to find out is from farm people themselves.

For many years, the pages of FARM JOURNAL have been a forum for the opinions, joys, sorrows, reflections, advice of country-wise men, women—and sometimes children. We've shared their experience and wisdom and humor and heartbreak with millions of other families who also earn their living and find their perspectives on the land.

Take the piece by Iowa farmer Clarence Hill on "How to Raise a Boy." Carroll Streeter, then Editor of FARM JOURNAL, was visiting the Hill farm to get a story on putting up silage.

7

"On his place I saw a pond, ponies, a baseball diamond—every kind of boy-amusement you could think of. But the Hill boys weren't playing, they were working, helping Dad and the hired man vaccinate feeder lambs."

Clearly, Streeter knew, this was a man who could tell us something about boys. The result was "the best article on boy-raising we ever printed." It is a reflection of the family feeling among readers of FARM JOURNAL over the years that prompted the Hills to share with the editors, 23 years later, a letter about their fortieth anniversary.

We still get requests for reprints of an article we printed 20 years ago. Written by a 42-year-old wife and mother of three who was dying of cancer, it was titled—by her—"My Last Wonderful Days." It was typical of Hazel Beck Andre that she would use her ebbing strength to write down her experiences because "it might help someone else face such a crisis."

It's a country tradition to help your neighbor. And some of our best articles were answers to a reader's plea for help. One month, we printed a despairing letter from a young farm wife:

"I work hard, day after day, go out very seldom. But I have so little to show for my work that in spite of everything I feel I've failed. Even my husband says, 'This house looks like you've been gone a week.'"

More than 1500 farm women responded with thoughtful letters—some ten pages long—full of sympathy and advice. These were distilled into one of the most practical and most helpful articles on "coping" that has ever been printed.

Our aim in "The Farmer's Wife" magazine within FARM JOURNAL was also our slogan: "A Good Life As Well As A Good Living." In this book, we've collected the best of the "good life" articles from FARM JOURNAL. The universal human wisdom is as pertinent as ever. These "lessons in living" are as valid and helpful today as when they were printed originally. Always, our aim was to raise readers' sights and help them cope with the everyday pressures. Some of the tools—the means—have changed, but basic goals and dreams are universal, timeless.

Over and over, readers tell us that a letter or article they saw in FARM JOURNAL made it possible for two people (or a whole family) to recognize themselves and move from talking about the article to talking to each other . . . really communicating.

It is a sign of our humanity that it helps to know there are others who have the same problems and pleasures we have . . . and are willing to share their ideas, their sympathy, their understanding.

—The Editors of FARM JOURNAL

A Good Life as Well as a Good Living
THE FARM

Contour Furrows

Now this is art, a lusty, vigorous thing!
No pastel-tinted water coloring,
No formless, tortured carving out of wood,
No oil-blobs, never to be understood,
Could equal this—as real as death and birth:
These curved plow-sweeps across the page of earth,
These scalloped ribbonings of brown and green
Stair-stepping down to willow's golden sheen.

The artist pauses, from the tractor seat
Surveys his work. Where sky and furrow meet
His masterpiece is joined to heaven now—
The land his palette, and his brush a plow.

Ruth DeLong Peterson

I come to visit Wendell Berry not believing he really is a farmer. Can you call yourself a farmer if you till only 12 acres? Does a farmer spend two days a week teaching creative writing at a university? Will a farmer sit down in the morning after chores and put on paper some of the finest poetry about farming since Robert Frost?

Wendell Berry does. This man I seek has left New York City for these obscure hills, and I want to find out reasons why he and so many others are leaving cities and going back to the land.

Can you call yourself
a farmer
if you till only 12 acres?

I see a young, droop-shouldered man, thin as a Kentucky Wonder pole bean, emerge from a barn along the road. He carries a bucket of milk and I figure I have found my man.

After I talk to him for awhile, I decide that if he is not a genuine farmer, then I don't know how to fill a grease gun. He speaks for the thousands of small farmers, the Class IV and V groups who, the statistics tell us, are not leaving the farm but are taking part-time jobs to stay on the land they love.

Berry also speaks as the conscience of commercial farmers who love the land too. And who often harbor doubts

---

The lines of poetry in this article are excerpted from FARMING: A HAND BOOK, copyright 1967, 1968, 1969, 1970 by Wendell Berry and reprinted by permission of Harcourt Brace Jovanovich, Inc.

about the direction farming takes in the face of economic facts of life.

I am tempted to say that he merely disguises himself as a writer or college professor once in awhile, but even that is not true. He's never in disguise. Whatever he does, he does as a farmer—if a farmer is somebody who always has farming on his mind.

"I started thinking about farming early, and I've been thinking about it too long to quit. When I lived in the city, I thought about farming."

> ... the man born to farming,
> Whose hands reach into the ground and sprout,
> To him, the soil is a divine drug.
> (from The Man Born to Farming)

"Nearly everything we eat comes from this place," Berry continues. "And so does most of our pleasure. With such a small acreage, we're dependent on outside income, of course. But I think you can say we make a considerable amount of our living here."

He smiles and a little mysteriously adds: "Come on. I'll show you what I mean."

For the next three hours, we walk Berry's little farm, one blade of grass at a time. Slowly, with a farmer's sense of wonder, he unfolds to me the amazingly self-subsistent world he has created.

Gardens, orchards, pasture. Hen house, corn crib, hog lot, cow barn, hayloft, repair shop, beehives. He takes me through a well-stocked root cellar he has recently constructed. He shows me a storage room hung with sugar-cured hams and shoulders, and furnished with huge freezers his wife has diligently filled. He points enthusiastically at the new, gleaming-clean privy he built with a composting chamber underneath instead of a septic tank. Until he has good evidence of its safety, he uses the compost only on ornamental plants, not food crops. "We think there shouldn't be any such thing as waste," he says. "Are you *completely* self-subsistent?" I ask. "Well, no," he answers. "I'm interested in more independent sources of power—solar energy, for example. And I'm interested in the possibility of producing methane gas for fuel from manure. They've done it in England."

Berry leads me up his steep hill pasture, lushly covered with a stand of clover. "This field was all bony with rocks when I started," he said.

> *In the dark of the moon, in flying snow,*
> *in the dead of winter,*
> *War spreading, families dying, the world*
> *in danger,*
> *I walk a rocky hillside, sowing clover.*
> (The poem, *February 2, 1968)*

We reach the top of the hill, stand silently, seeing, in one sweep, miles of green valley. A pleasant view made extraordinary by the poet standing beside me. I know this as one of his writing places; I remember especially his poem, *On a Hill Late at Night:*

> *I am wholly willing to be here*
> *Between the bright silent thousands of stars*
> *And the life of the grass pouring out of the ground.*
> *The hill has grown to me like a foot.*
> *Until I lift the earth, I cannot move.*

I am wholly willing to be there, too, with this man who lifts the commonplaces of farming to heights of artistic beauty. I keep thinking about how I had always wanted to walk with Frost or Sandburg over their farms. But this is even better. Wendell Berry is my age, his poetry touches my secret places.

"I am trying to demonstrate with a semi-subsistence farm that incorporates the best of traditional agriculture

14

with a selective use of new technology that *more* people can live on the land, not fewer," Berry explains. "Technology has been geared to bigness; it must now be turned to serve *the individual,* too. I am a Jeffersonian. I see the small farmers leaving the land; I see small business closing down in dying villages. People are herding together in cities where they are controlled by an ever more powerful monolithic bureaucracy. As we lose our self-sufficiency, we lose our freedom."

Berry knows something about cities. In 1962, after having lived for two years on the West Coast and in Europe for a year, he accepted a teaching position at New York University. "That was what a writer was supposed to do—go to New York.

"But I was not satisfied. I hungered for something I cannot yet quite put in words. What is it about the farm that once experienced, never leaves you? I was uprooted. But it was more than that. The disease of the city is nonentity.

"A man familiar with his *place,* a place in which he can measure himself against existence, begins to understand who he is. The people leaving the cities are looking for that kind of familiarity.

"They want a place they can invest their lives in, not just their money. They're fed up with the assumption that everything equals money. They've realized many of the best things can't be bought, but have to be worked for."

Berry's eyes seem to shelter quiet anger as he stares off the rim of his hill. You have to look closely for the humor behind them.

"When I decided to leave New York, some faculty members said I was making a bad mistake. There are still a lot of people who quote Thomas Wolfe's 'You Can't Go Home Again' and believe it.

"I had to come back home and live for three years before I realized just how foolish and destructive that idea

15

is. My city friends used to worry that I would get fat and join the Farm Bureau," Berry smiles.

"The really amusing thing is that New York is one of the most provincial places on earth."

We descend the hill, by way of a dry creek bed in a wood. In the barn, he tosses an ear of corn to his two hogs. "For a really good ham, a hog should fatten slowly, without all this modern efficiency." He doesn't explain that. He expects me to understand.

We move down to the riverbank. I have seen his farm. It is time now to think about it. Berry hunkers down on a rock and looks at the water rolling by. I skip flat rocks across the water.

The people leaving the cities want a place they can invest their lives in, not just their money.

"You see," he finally says, "most businessmen would think this is simply crazy. My subsistence farm produces life but no profits, so it is work for nothing. No GNP, you see. We are conditioned to judge all things by profit and loss. That's the reality my ideals must struggle with every day. City people visit me and they all want to be farmers.

"Isn't that *amazing*. They don't want to be farmers— they just want to be *themselves* and the life they lead won't allow it. I tell them right away: I make a salary from teaching. They have to be warned that mere subsistence is no way to live, at least not in this country now. And they have to learn what I do is *hard work*.

"I want to be called an organic farmer. I'm not a purist

about organics, but that's where I want to stand. If enough people would take hold of a small piece of land and love it like I try to do, wouldn't America be improved ecologically *and* socially?

"If that puts me among the crackpots, so be it. I'm for the agricultural renegades and for whatever it takes to remind science and business of the gross commercialism that is doing violence to the land, and to people's lives.

"Organics is not just about using chemicals or not using chemicals. That's the narrow view. Organics is talking about a *shift in power*. We want more control over our own *lives*—at the local level. Washington, D.C., cannot take care of us, nor can General Electric nor can IT&T. We are trying to make a kind of life that's not totally dependent on a salary and on the corporations."

He glances at his watch. Choretime. He picks up his milk bucket, and heads for the barn to milk his two cows by hand.

> *I am not bound for any public place,*
> *but for ground of my own*
> *Where I have planted vines*
> *and orchard trees,*
> *and in the heat of the day climbed up*
> *into the healing shadow*
> *of the woods.*
> *Better than any argument*
> *is to rise at dawn and pick*
> *dew-wet red berries in a cup.*
> *(From A Standing Ground)*

—*Gene Logsdon*

*F*armers are found in fields—plowing up, seeding down, rotating from, planting to, fertilizing with, spraying for and harvesting if. Wives help them, little boys follow them, the Agriculture Department confuses them, city relatives visit them, salesmen detain them, meals wait for them, weather can delay them, but it takes Heaven to stop them.

When your car stalls along the way, a farmer is a considerate, courteous, inexpensive road service. When a farmer's wife suggests he buy a new suit, he can quote from memory every expense involved in operating the farm last year plus the added expenses he is certain will crop up this year. Or else he assumes the role of the indig-

---

What is a farmer?
"Nobody else is so far from the phone or so close to God."

---

nant shopper, impressing everyone within earshot the pounds of pork he must produce in order to pay for a suit at today's prices.

A farmer is a paradox—he is an overalled executive with his home his office; a scientist using fertilizer attachments; a purchasing agent in an old straw hat; a personnel director with grease under his fingernails; a dietician with a passion for alfalfa, aminos and antibiotics; a production expert faced with a surplus, and a manager battling a price-cost squeeze. He manages more capital than most of the businessmen in town.

He likes sunshine, good food, State Fairs, dinner at *noon*, auctions, his neighbors, Saturday nights in town, his shirt collar unbuttoned and, above all, a good soaking rain in August.

He is not much for drouths, ditches, throughways, experts, weeds, the eight-hour day, helping with housework, or grasshoppers.

Nobody else is so far from the telephone or so close to God. Nobody else gets so much satisfaction out of modern plumbing, good weather and homemade ice cream. Nobody else has in his pockets at one time a three-bladed knife, checkbook, a billfold, a pair of pliers and a combination memo book and general farm guide.

Nobody else can remove these things from his pockets and, on washday, have overlooked: five "steepes," one cotter key, a rusty spike, three grains of corn, the stub end of a lead pencil, a square tap, a $4.98 pocket watch and a cupful of chaff in each trouser cuff.

A farmer is both Faith and Fatalist—he must have faith to continually meet the challenges of his capacities amid an ever-present possibility that an act of God (a late spring, an early frost, tornado, flood, drouth) can bring his business to a standstill. You can *reduce his acreage* but you can't *restrain his ambition.*

Might as well put up with him—he is your friend, your competitor, your customer, your source of food, fiber, and self-reliant young citizens to help replenish your cities. He is your countryman—a denim-dressed, business-wise, fast-growing statesman of stature. And when he comes in at noon having spent the energy of his hopes and dreams, he can be recharged anew with the magic words on the radio: "The market's up!"

—Doris T. West

*L*ooking back to the time when my husband and I decided to move to a Virginia farm, I can hardly believe how naive I was. To me a farm was one of those lovely green places we sometimes passed during a Sunday afternoon drive. Our approach to this one—the farm we had acquired—unrolled an idyllic view: freshly mowed hayfields (what impressive machinery!); a picturesque red barn casting its shadow on the hillside; cows grazing—or gazing out over the fences. . . .

For ten years now I've been on the cows' side of the fence. (I have come to envy the cattle; they have so much

---

For ten years, I've been on the cows' side of the fence.

---

time!) I know it will take days of labor to get the hay in from those idyllic fields, and I've become more concerned with how much baled hay that picturesque barn contains than with the shadow it casts.

By now I am sure that the power will go off at times, usually when it's most critically needed. I stay braced for the inevitable week when our pressure pump won't perform and some town friends I've invited for *sometime* arrive *now* "to stay a few days." It is during such crises that Bill or Win, our twins, will add havoc to confusion—like the time Win broke an arm falling out of a tree, when we had fruit to put up and the freezer went haywire.

Our farm, once a showplace, had been going steadily to the dogs for 20 years before we took it over. After owning it half that long, we're still in the Reconstruction Period. Or maybe we are in our own Hundred Years War—against broken fences, weeds that grow five times as fast as the crops, egg-stealing snakes. . . .

Plus deposits in the living room of whatever crop is being harvested: oats on the sofa, lespedeza on the rug, alfalfa in the armchair. And mud! Year round, tracked in, swept out, mopped up, scraped off our shoes and washed out of clothes. When I agreed to move out here to this farm, I didn't realize I'd have to live in the same house with it!

Moving from city to farm, a woman may miss the familiar pattern of near neighbors, frequent shopping, hours spent in the library, at movies and concerts. I still miss those things (not that they aren't available; too often *I'm* not available). But who in the city gets serenaded nightly by a resident mockingbird?

From my kitchen window I see, not clustered houses and tall buildings surrounded by trafficky streets, but long distances—green in spring and summer, brown in fall, white in winter. An unbroken view of the Blue Ridge Mountains has shaped my philosophy. When, after some chore, I raise my eyes to those hills, I tell them silently: "Your greatness is partly mine, because I feel it deep inside myself; because I work for and earn the right to enjoy your misty purple mornings and glowing sunsets."

My husband and I both know that we'll never move back to the other side of the fence—to the city side. For that matter, if you should stop by tomorrow, likely you'd find me hard at work painting my side!

—*Maryon Wood Harper*

*W*hen Bruce and I moved to this ranch, we arrived in a truck. I didn't get right down from my high seat. "I think I'll just stay out here and enjoy it all," I told my husband.

Holding our fast-asleep baby, and conscious of the 2- and 4-year- olds tumbling out on the ground like puppies, I just sat there—breathing in and listening.

The evening was pure mountain spring. The sun had warmed the pines that day and their sharp scent filled the air. Small, busy sounds punctuated the stillness: sleepy birds twittering, a distant cow bell . . . I sensed,

---

City visitors ask, "How do you stand the stillness?" But to our finely tuned ears, the silence is laced with sound.

---

rather than saw, that the gray remains of snow were trickling away in miniature creeks; but I heard clearly the muted voices of these little streams.

Always my keenest awarenesses have been of smells and sounds—the essences and undertones of our life on the ranch. My nostrils and ears have learned to recognize a pattern—for instance, the acrid odor of disinfectant means that a hurt or sick animal is receiving attention. A coyote's barking nearby (might send a frightened colt running into barbed wire) . . . the smell of smoke where smoke shouldn't be . . . such signals send us on the double, to investigate.

Probably the most panicking "sound" is silence, when there should be undertones of children at play. A ranch is not the safest place in the world for small boys. Many's the moment I've questioned myself suddenly: *How long since I heard them? Which way could they have gone?* (I'll never forget the time our 5-year-old disappeared. It was spring, and the river was high, and we were terrified. But finally the "runaway" was found—asleep in a closet!)

Often when the wind blows, it touches only the tops of the giant pines so that the high branches toss and moan while the air at our level is perfectly still. In early spring one may be listening to just such a wind when another sound intrudes. The river, long muffled under winter's ice, has broken forth to add its voice to the season's symphony. Because it usually breaks up at night, only once have we watched the ice go out. An unforgettable sight: massive chunks roaring by on torrential waters that carried trees, bridges, all kinds of debris. . . .

Through the summer the river settles down, minds its manners and murmurs politely past our back door. Summer always smells of hot pine pitch, of peppermint crushed underfoot and of wild flowers. An evening thunder shower assails the senses . . . fragrances of sprinkled-down dust and clean vegetation blend with accompanying sounds—rumble and clap of thunder, the rush of rain.

Summer also brings the smell of hay drying in hot sun; the bawling and yelling noises of cattle drives, the shouts of children home for vacation. Children imitate sounds of animals and machinery, such as stampeding cattle, whooshing jet planes. Their smells are of the horses they ride, the dirt they dig, the trees they climb and the ferns they roll in.

Autumn's crisp, cool days usher in the crackle of flames in the wood stove, the chatter of birds ready to fly south. We all wear the orchard's appley fragrance—even my husband. Bruce's characteristic aroma the year around is of horses and saddle leather; but he varies this according to season—including smells of tractor fuel and freshly

23

turned earth, the burnt-hair smell of branding time, the odor of snow-dampened wool. His sounds, softened by laughter and affection, are commanding ones: the peculiar shrill whistle with which he summons dog, horse or sons; his voice of fatherly authority.

In the winter . . . did you ever hear falling snow? Listen closely, for the sound is as soft as a whisper. It promises a snug time of sharing for the family, and it foretells a bountiful crop-growing season.

City visitors ask Bruce and me, "How do you stand the stillness up here?" But to our finely tuned ears the silence is laced with sound. And ranch smells, some of which offend city noses, are barometers—helping measure our valley's moods. I hope that the work of ranching will never rob us of our special awarenesses.

—*Beth L. Beck*

A three-acre patch tucked in the corner of my north 80 has never felt a plow or produced a salable crop. Sounds like pretty shaky management, but that plot is virgin prairie, and to me the most valuable land on the farm. Our kids wander through the coarse grass and fragile flowers and occasionally probe for Indian artifacts. Classes from local schools, a few tourists, old-timers and botanists regard my prairie as a living example of the past.

It's easy to get sentimental about this kind of unretouched nature that once carpeted three quarters of the Corn Belt. But virgin prairie can't be fully appreciated from a distance: You have to get involved. The grass has an odor midway between sweet and musty, and feels like elegant carpet underfoot. In mid-summer, wild aster, blazing star, yellow cone flower and many others spatter the terrain with haphazard color. There are interesting plants like the compass flower, whose leaves always grow in a north-south direction. The prairie changes every day from May till late fall. From adjacent fields, it's an arresting end-row oasis.

But my private prairie has more than sentimental or poetic value. Several agronomists have visited it. The Iowa State University Botany Department has identified more than 60 kinds of flowers and grasses that thrive only in such uncultivated fields. Outside of a few state-owned prairies, this unkempt vegetation has survived only in scattered spots along railroad rights-of-way and a few country graveyards. Scientists say this undisturbed soil yields many chemical and entomological secrets. In other words, there's no shortage of crop land, but native prairie is becoming scarce.

Early one spring, the ISU botanists burned off about a third of my favorite field for a regrowth experiment. I was a bit apprehensive, but the green plants emerged through the charred residue within days, much as they did a century ago when prairie fires swept through.

A string of tile and a couple hours' plowing would make my virgin prairie produce a whopping yield of corn. But once you turn it over there's no turning back. So I guess there's more than one way to measure the land's yield. The way a neighbor put it: "It took the Lord a thousand years to raise that crop; no use you trying to do better."

—*Rex Gogerty*

The Beginning Years
LOVE AND MARRIAGE

On Sharing

Sharing begins with hosts of little things:
A poem read, the rising of the sun
Across a lake, telling how some bird sings,
Climbing a hill together for the fun
Of standing, side by side, upon its crest;
Giving a gift, bringing good news, for it
Is better shared, and laughter shared is blest.
Day in, day out, and slowly bit by bit,
Sharing begins unconsciously with no
Thought of return except another's pleasure—
But mark how often it's been known to grow
Until the sharing of the heart's dear treasure
Is so compelling two become aware
How true their love is by their need to share.

Elaine V. Emans

Dearly beloved,

we are gathered together here in the sight of God and in the presence of these witnesses...

Since I started out as a country preacher I have piloted many couples through the marriage service used in our church. And sometimes I get a futile feeling as I read the solemn lines—as if I were talking to myself!

I observe that my two star performers are in an impenetrable daze. . . ."I had stage fright so bad I didn't know what was going on," the girl may confide later; and from the boy: "All I could hear was my knees knocking."

If the couple has been to me for some counseling, I probably don't worry so much about them as about the rest of the people at the wedding. Everyone gets so interested in the beauty of the bride, the nervousness of the groom or the cunning antics of the flower girl that the deeper meanings seem to roll off. And that bothers me!

For we all have a stake in this. Marriage is not a private affair, but a contract involving at least four parties: a man, a woman, God and the community. All can rejoice in the happy union of the two who are in love; all will be hurt if the marriage muddles along, mires down or breaks up.

So it's to many people I'm speaking—these prospective partners, also brides and grooms of the future, parents, and the community at large—as I read the service. . .

To join this man and this woman in holy matrimony. . .

Because the familiar words of the ritual come easily to me, I'm prone to send out some silent companion-thoughts. To this girl in white, and her man: Do you feel the solemnity—do you realize that here is something that really is *holy?*

When you cast your lives together under this contract, you become particular instruments of God's love. You may honorably share with Him the mystery and miracle of creation. Your children, born in His image, will work, play, love and worship—like you, according to your example. So your marriage is sacred in a very special way.

It is therefore not to be entered into unadvisedly...
The couple before me has likely done some soul-searching, perhaps under my guidance, and are off to a promising start. In any case, the die is cast for them, barring a sudden retreat at the altar.

But these lines are important to everyone here—you parents, leaders, all you grown-ups to whom youngsters look for the answers. Help them to understand:

No couple should marry until they've thought the matter through maturely, learned much about themselves and each other. Marriage isn't a picnic for a day—it's a pact "so long as ye both shall live." Give yourselves a time of courtship—long enough to make sure there are no basic conflicts that could destroy your marriage. Enough time and thought keeps love from being blind.

Into this holy estate come two persons now to be joined.
Joined is a strong word. This pair shall be two no longer, but one. They will see their oneness in the faces of their children; they will hear someone say, "She has her mother's eyes and her father's nose."

But being "one" sometimes turns into a struggle of individuals to decide *which* one! It should be a blending of the best in each; the best talents, best tolerance; the most all-cherishing and freely-expressed love. We can all help this blending, by recognizing the best in each partner.

If the solemn vows you are about to take be kept inviolate...
There is no way to be almost true. So any vow that is

kept is kept inviolate—unviolated. It cannot be smudged even a little bit.

No one is perfect, and you will fail each other in many ways. You will forgive and be forgiven. But *wilfully or irresponsibly* failing each other is breaking faith.

Failure to keep marriage vows is not limited to sexual infidelity. Both husbands and wives can be unfaithful in other ways: by nagging or belittling; by listening to gossip or criticism about a partner; by withholding the self—failing to confide, to listen, to share.

No other ties more tender...

A strange mystery is that these tender marriage-bonds can be the strongest on earth. Yet they are most easily

---

The wedding ring may be the strongest thing of its size in the world.

---

broken by small, habitual annoyances—or by outside interference. *Let none put asunder* is an admonition for neighbors, friends—and for the parents of the young marrieds.

John, wilt thou have this woman to be thy wedded wife...
Love her...

I've known many a man who loved his wife sure enough, but didn't seem to like her very well. He didn't want to exchange ideas with her about the farm business or home planning; didn't like to talk with her about community issues, politics or world affairs; didn't offer to take her fishing or hunting. And he couldn't be bothered with "trivialities"—the cake she baked for Club, or the book she laughed and cried over.

What kind of love is that? The kind most women could do without!

Comfort her. . . lend a solid shoulder for her to weep on; or help her get back her perspective when she cries for no good reason. . .

Honor and keep her. . . keep strong the note of pride when you introduce her to strangers: "This is *my wife!*". . . Bite your tongue in two before you'll say a disrespectful word about her.

In sickness and in health. . . but obviously, you say? Nevertheless, chronic ill health is said to be one of the biggest obstacles to marriage happiness. The saving trick is to put health in its place—to make loving allowances for illness without letting it rule.

And, forsaking all others, keep thee only unto her so long as ye both shall live?
This doesn't mean, of course, that you two shall live apart from the world—in a cave or on an island. Workably interpreted, forsaking all others means avoiding any attachment—not just romantic—that could hurt or belittle your mate. It means putting your marriage ahead of all outside interests—parents, pals, work, your favorite hobby. A man can betray his wife by spending all his spare time with the TV set!

I Mary, take thee John, to be my wedded husband, to have and to hold, from this day forward, for better, for worse, for richer, for poorer. . .
To have the undivided love of a good man is to be rich, no matter what the bank statement may say. But on the practical side, you and your man should by now have thought this through together: Just how important is it to each of you that he be a "good provider"? One of you may have more ambitious goals than the other. Believing dif-

ferently cannot destroy your marriage; but it could be wrecked by nagging, or by either indicating that the other isn't quite adequate at living, loving, or keeping up with the Joneses.

In sickness and in health, to love and to cherish till death do us part...

You and John have now taken the same vows and assumed equal responsibility. Keep your love the star by which he sets his course. Let him see in your eyes and hear in your voice that you think he is wonderful. For your pride in him is necessary to his pride in himself—and without that he can't progress or achieve.

When you wash and bake and sew and clean, do not say this is drudgery, but "This is my love made meaningful and real." You can say the same when you walk out on housekeeping to go to the cattle sale with your husband, or to enjoy some time alone with yourself.

The wedding ring is an outward and visible symbol of an inward and spiritual bond...

It is only a symbol, of course. Without inward and spiritual fidelity, all symbols are meaningless. The flag is just a piece of bright cloth; the cross is no more than a bit of wood or metal; the wedding ring is merely jewelry.

But worn with sturdy, unqualified loyalty, and with cherishing, the wedding ring may be the strongest thing of its size in the world. Our civilization, built on the family, would fall apart except for the bond that unites two hearts in endless love.

—Don Ian Smith

*T*he average farmer is a champion among worriers. He frets about uncooperative weather, high taxes, the cost-price squeeze and how to make a good livelihood.

As a result, the farmer's wife needs to be one of the listeningest persons in the world. Her husband, without quite meaning to, often finds himself astraddle the kitchen stool spilling over with troubles. She knows that bottling up his worries can lead to ulcers, so she hears the man out.

But listen between the lines! One of the trickiest things I had to learn as a farmer's bride was to detect the

---

I learned the difference between Bill's real worries and his routine grousing.

---

difference between Bill's real worries and his routine grousing.

I label it "routine" when he complains that planting season came so late, we'll end up with 100 acres of fodder and no corn; or that our cows have forgotten how to have anything but bull calves.

But often the farmer has real cause for headaches. Rust can reduce a wheat field to a stand of empty heads. Cows that refuse to freshen play hob with the milk base. A single rain can make the difference between profit and no profit. Excessive worry hinders constructive thinking; so a concerned wife looks for ways to ease the man's mind.

There are some things not to do! Don't call attention to a neighbor who has twice the trouble. Knowing John Jones lost his best cow doesn't alter the fact that our alfalfa winter-killed. I know one wife who tries to laugh away her husband's worries; another who simply walks out of the room. Either method discourages communication—and anxiety needs to be talked out.

I have tried matching each of Bill's worries with one of my own. That does not help his mood either. It only doubles his load when I point out that the washing machine has quit again. Besides, he might remind me I'm prone to over-stuff the washer.

So mostly I just listen. But I may work in a casual question—one that I know has a favorable answer. When Bill frets that unseasonable weather is causing the oats to ripen without filling, I ask him about the corn. He has to admit that it never looked better—and the first thing we know, he has talked himself out of his gloom.

He honors one request of mine—that worry talk be confined to daylight. It used to be that after convincing me we were heading for bankruptcy, he'd roll over and sleep, leaving me to stare into the dark till morning. At breakfast I would be in no shape to rejoice when he'd rush in and announce, "Trixie's got a new heifer calf—a beauty!"

There is no monopoly on helpful listening—it works both ways. When our purebred sow died last winter, a week before she was to farrow, I sat on a bale and cried. My partner offered me a barny-smelling shoulder and reasoned that we'd been having fair luck with the stock and the law of averages was bound to catch up with us. I'll never make a habit of crying, though, for my husband views a weeping woman with the same enthusiasm he has for a stand of thistles.

The competent farmer's motto, although unspoken, must be kin to the 4-H slogan "to make the best better." He simply can't let it rest when anything stands between him and that bumper crop, those top-notch cows or a load of prime hogs. He may have to settle for less than the best, but don't expect him not to worry about it!

Non-worry can be suspect. Awhile back I mentioned a farmer whom we know slightly—that he seemed so care-free. Bill took me for a drive past the man's place, in order to show me that his fence posts were leaning like rickrack.

Maybe it takes some fretting just to keep the place up. At any rate, as long as my husband is in the business he loves, he will have anxieties. And as he airs them, I'll offer medicine that's time-tried.

I will be on hand—listening.

—*Minnesota Farm Wife*

THOUGHT FOR YOUR
WEDDING DAY

If every husband would take as much trouble to focus on his own small failings as he does to getting a clear picture on TV . . . And if he'd cheer as loudly over his wife's apple pies as he does at the ball game . . . And if every wife would cook for her husband as painstakingly as she does for her club . . . and work as hard "getting an angle" on his interests as she does getting a just-right tilt to her hat . . . And if both would sometimes make believe they were living in front of a picture window, and had a live microphone broadcasting what they say . . .

Why, Reno would be just another village in Nevada!

Minnesota Farm Wife

A little boy on a farm in Oregon heard his parents quarreling. Afterward his mother was unhappy, so he tried to comfort her: "Mommy, you know Daddy really loves you. He just doesn't like you." The story brings a chuckle; but it is sobering to reflect what a widespread and ironic truth that child put his finger on. There is evidence that half the marriages in the U.S. are just tolerable; the partners "love" each other, but they aren't very good friends.

Are most farm couples happy? *Some* are. Farm marriages are supposed to be the stable ones. But many letters from rural addresses admit disappointment. For example: "My husband looks at me as if I weren't there. He remembers anniversaries, but I would trade every routine gift for just one spontaneous compliment, or even a friendly wink now and then."

"Mommy, you know Daddy really loves you. He just doesn't like you."

Some people argue that love and love alone will keep a marriage alive and healthy; that if a husband and wife "really love" each other, they will get along all right. This is oversimplifying; it is only part of the truth. In a marriage doing its whole job the couple can say to each other, and mean it: "I love you, and what's more I *like* you!"

The love and friendship combination is more important than ever in these modern times, for marriage has changed and expanded in purpose. In earlier generations a man had to have a mate to bear his children and help

36

work his fields. Today marriage still has its practical side (the farmer still needs a wife to help run his business). But it must go further and deeper: *It must help the man and the woman grow—in spirit, in accomplishment, in sensitivity.*

If I looked for people who would disagree with that last statement, probably I couldn't find enough to fill a phone booth. But I'd find many husbands and wives who would say quite desperately: "Marriage isn't like that for us. How can we make it so?"

There are no pat answers, of course. But I would suggest: It will be a step in the right direction if both you and your partner can face the lacks in your marriage and work on them together. (Too often it's up to just one to make all the moves.)

Can the two of you talk things over during a relaxed interlude? Ask yourselves: *What is love, and what is friendship?*

Actually, love and friendship are akin, and they should be almost inseparable. Both involve enjoyment of and concern for another person—the beloved, the friend.

We think of love as being profound and tender (although it can be delightfully zany). Love in marriage is an intimate relationship that includes emotional closeness, enjoyment of sex, eagerness to give and receive pleasure of various kinds.

Friendship is more matter-of-fact—more intellectual. Friendship in marriage is putting your minds together as well as your physical and spiritual selves. It is sharing some special interests—reading, music, politics, farm sales, sports. . . . It's also granting freedom for each to have some separate interests. It is *liking each other!*

What's to be done if neither love nor friendship seems to have survived? You can't turn on dried-up feelings like water from a spigot.

You can try—by agreement, if possible—to practice ex-

37

tra considerateness and thoughtfulness. Good manners help people feel in harmony—even husbands and wives!

For a start, try asking some silent questions (mentally addressed to your wife or husband):

• How long has it been since I said "I love you" (or responded to those words from you)?

• Have I invited you lately (or eagerly accepted your invitation) to a movie or to have dinner out?

• How long since we read a book together—or a magazine article? How long since we gabbed back and forth about something—a TV play, Civil Rights, politics?

• Do I ever beam with pride, or brag to the neighbors, over something you've accomplished? (The talk you gave at PTA, the desk you built for our 8-year-old.)

• How long since I encouraged you to do something you wanted to do (or am I usually the wet blanket)? . . . How long since I really listened—with heart as well as ears—when you wanted to talk?

When you have asked those silent questions, the answers you supply should point out ways to be more thoughtful and considerate. You may even feel stirrings of an old tenderness.

Will it all add up to new happiness in your marriage? There's no guarantee, of course. But you've nothing to lose by trying—and everything to gain.

— *H. Del Schalock, Ph.D.*
Associate Professor of Family Life,
Oregon State University
with Maude Longwell

*H*ow can I get my husband to change? John just will not face up to his inefficiency in farming and do something about it. The first year we were married, our net income was under $500. We had no disasters, either; John's normal farming produced our practically invisible income, and matters haven't changed in the eight years since. I'm at my wits' end. . . .

Should you try to remodel your mate?

I started reading farm magazines, and sent to State University for agricultural bulletins. I urged my husband to go with me to farm meetings. For a city woman who hadn't known the difference between a sow and a shoat, I learned a lot about pigs. Finally, last year, I persuaded John to let me bring up one litter my way. Those pigs went to market at age five months—brought top price.

But my husband continues in the same old rut. Last fall he lost 10 pigs from just five litters. I think they died of malnutrition. I try to convince John that creep feed plus extra protein costs less in the long run because pigs are ready to sell earlier. But he's not impressed.

The truth is, my husband borders on being lazy. He'll walk around a log rather than remove it from the path. He spends hours reading literary magazines which we can't afford, but he will not read articles on better methods of feeding or castrating.

Now don't blame our problem on "lack of communication"! My husband and I have no trouble discussing the situation. Incidentally, John has many fine qualities. He is superior to me intellectually. He is amiable and outgoing, which makes him popular with our neighbors and

friends. But all this doesn't provide us with a living.
Could anyone blame a wife for nagging?
                                              —Mary S.

Why does a woman who values success marry a non-provider in the first place? Marrying someone who is "made to be made over" is a trap which has ensnared many a strong-minded person of whichever sex.

The problem which Mary describes does go deeper than lack of communication, as she observes. It also goes deeper than her husband's inefficiency and the inadequate income. John is still the man Mary chose to marry nearly eight years ago. But something has happened to him. Into his life has come a woman who wants to love and accept him, but at the price of changing his basic nature.

Trying to make another person into your idealized image of what he ought to be is, actually, a kind of self-love. Mary is projecting on her amiable, easy-going, bookish, improvident husband her image of his exact opposite: a "successful" man—aggressive, driving, red-blooded. It's simply not his nature to be such a person, I suspect. She had better accept him as he is—or leave him.

The opposite of "accept" is "reject." Mary has rejected her husband from the start, because unconsciously she married him for what she thought she could make him into. She rejects him now, over and over, because she cannot change him. Supposing John did try to change to become the somebody else his wife specifies. Would the farm operation pick up? I doubt John could change that much. He would fail for two reasons: first, because a person of mature age can't change his whole personality; second, no one can ever become the imaginary person made up of another person's deep psychological needs.

There is a basic rule about human nature. No one changes by someone else changing him. But if you can accept him as he is, and let him be secure and comfortable with what he is, you can free him (and yourself) from exhausting conflict. The energies he would use up in trying to preserve the self he is can then be used for changing *some*, and for growing somewhat.

You have to accept him without reservation, though. How often during a counseling session have I heard the indignant outburst: "But I've accepted him (or her) for three months, and he (she) hasn't changed a bit!" Deep down, the offending mate recognizes that the acceptance has strings attached, and resists changing all the harder.

Show me the man and wife who really share in their marriage, and I'll show you a couple who have accepted each other—strengths *and* limitations. With that mutual security, each can afford to face up to his weaknesses and his mate's strengths without losing face.

From my own growing-up in the country, I feel that the farm is a natural place to "grow" acceptance. Children are valued cogs in the family machinery. The habit of sharing—chores, responsibilities, rewards—gradually weaves itself into the personality. And to share is to accept.

—Dr. Aaron L. Rutledge
Head of Counseling Services and Psychotherapy,
Merrill-Palmer Institute, Detroit

THE LAST NOTE

After writing thank-you notes for baby gifts, I wondered if I had forgotten anyone. Suddenly, it dawned on me that one of the most thoughtful and helpful persons was my husband Ken. He sent me flowers, visited me faithfully, had the house neat when I came home, and promptly pitched in with diapers, formula and feedings. I addressed my biggest thank-you note to him—to tell him how very special he is to me.

Sandy Stevens

41

*O*ptimism," according to Ambrose Bierce, "is an intellectual disorder yielding to no treatment but death." He should also have said that it is a trait predominately female.

It seems ever to have been the lot of woman to choke back her tears and say, "Never mind, honey, something good is bound to happen," even when honey is listening to a ball game instead of looking for work, and she has just found weevils in the last sack of cornmeal.

I don't know why most females are optimists; neither do I know why all males are pessimists. I do know that it has nothing to do with nationality, because we have right in our immediate family one Scotch, one Danish, one German, one English, and one Swedish saddo (family word for pessimist) who can hardly wait to get home at night to hand out their sodden lumps of bad news or to prophesy a black future. To my side of the family, Gabriel Heatter with his "bad news tonight" was not exceptional. He was just a husband who's on the radio.

I was born an optimist, inherited from Mother no doubt.

I was born an optimist, inherited from Mother no doubt, and if it is the only intellectual disorder I ever harbor I shall consider myself fortunate. Optimism has taken me through some very tough times. And even though singing "It's a Lovely Day Today" as you bail the water out of the flooded basement may not be the answer for everyone, burying your head in your arms and bawling isn't either.

Take that time six months or so after I wrote *The Egg and I.* It was a lovely day, a June morning, and Don and I were on our way to the Washington town, Vashon, to get groceries. Not very many, either, as we had exactly $2.81 and pay day wasn't until Monday. As we neared the top of the hill I said, "Let's stop and get the mail." "Why?" Don asked in his low, sad, Scotch voice.

"Because there might be good news," I said.

"Humph," Don said, driving past the mail box.

"Oh, come on," I said. "Stop. Let's get the mail."

"It'll only be bills we can't pay," Don said.

"I have a feeling something good might happen," I said.

"You have that feeling every morning," Don said, but he did stop and back up. In the mailbox there was an air-mail letter containing a check for $750. We celebrated later, the females hugging and shouting: "See, I told you so. Something good always happens!" while the men talked about the dollar being worth only 50 cents.

Then there was that awful bleak period during the depression when none of us had jobs. For days and days we had hung dispiritedly around the house watching the rain splat against the windows, burning books in the furnace, looking hungrily at our pet mallard duck. Then one raw morning as she used the last scoop of coffee Mother said, "Now, things can't get any worse so they'll have to get better." And that was the morning the postman brought Mother and me each $50 prizes in a slogan-writing contest.

I'll never forget the day I was admitted to a sanatorium and watched the doctor write on my card, "Pulmonary tuberculosis, prognosis—doubtful." Not even daring to think of my two little girls, I asked timidly, how long he thought I'd have to stay there. "Year at least. Probably much, much longer," he said. Quickly Mother said, "Nonsense, Betsy. You come from a long line of healthy people. Do what they say and be cheerful and you'll be home before you know it." Nine months and 27 pounds later I was released from the sanatorium and have been in excellent health ever since.

After the war, Don and I bought a 10-acre farm on Vashon Island. There we gradually acquired six dairy cows of assorted breeds; two ewes and a ram; two sows (one of which always ate her pigs); 5000 chickens; a few ducks and geese; and a succession of dolorous farmers—one of whom wore a sun helmet and sang Calypso songs in French, one who read bad news in the papers by the egg candling light, but not one who ever gave us a jot of good news.

One clear spring afternoon when I was out planting my ranunculuses and being glad that I was alive, the phone rang. Merton, our then-time farmer, said, "Say, Betty, got a shotgun handy?"

"No," I said, "Why?"

"Redwater!" he said dramatically.

"Redwater?" I said. "What's that?"

"You'll see," he said. "The Brown Swiss cow has it bad, and we might as well shoot the rest and get it over with."

"Where's Don?" I asked.

"Oh, he's went to town to get some kind of real strong medicine for the chickens. We're lookin' for Newcastle to wipe out the *hull* flock."

"Well, listen," I said. "Don't shoot anybody or anything until Don gets home. I'll call the veterinarian."

"Call if you want," he said, "but 'twon't do any good."

The veterinarian came over on the 5 o'clock boat, immediately diagnosed the cow's trouble, opened up two or three of her stomachs, removed some undigested baling wire, threw in some sulfa powder, sewed her up, and in a week she was as good as ever. The chickens didn't get Newcastle disease either, surprising Merton and Don who had counted on it.

Another time Ellsworthy, the one who read bad news by

the egg candling light, called at six in the morning and gasped into the phone, "Tell Don that something has got into the 1080! The stuff's all over the barn floor, the dogs are foaming at the mouth, the chickens are all dying, the pigs will go next, and he'd better git up there."

"What is 1080?" I asked.

"One of the deadliest of poisons known to man and issued only by government permit, that's all," he said, slamming down the phone.

Vaulting up the stairs I yelled at Don, who was in the shower, "Ellsworthy just called, and he says that there is 1080 all over the barn, the dogs are foaming at the mouth, the chickens are all dying and the pigs will go next."

"What in heck is 1080?" Don asked.

"Just the deadliest of poisons known to man and issued only by government permit, that's all," I snapped. "You'd better hurry."

The phone was ringing again. I tore down the stairs and jerked off the receiver. Ellsworthy panted: "Tell Don to bring some lard and soda and I'll try to save his dogs for him anyway."

I was out of soda and I couldn't find any lard so I thrust a new can of Crisco and some rock salt (I found in the grindy ice cream freezer) into Don's arms as he raced out the door. Then I put on the coffee and tried to remember where I had seen something about a terrible new poison. As I searched through the dusty recesses of my mind, the coffee boiled over and drooled down the front of the stove. I pushed it back to settle, wiped up the spillings, then poured two cups and went into Mother's room.

Handing her a cup I said, "Everything on the farm is dead or dying." Yawning, Mother said, "More redwater?" "No, this time it sounds serious," I said and told her all about 1080.

Sipping her coffee, Mother said, "That Ellsworthy! It's ridiculous. Why it would take 50 gallons of anything just to wet the barn floor."

I said, "But Ellsworthy said that the dogs are foaming at the mouth and half the chickens are dead already."

"Humph," Mother said. "He probably read some article last night when he was supposed to be candling eggs."

When Don finally called to tell me that a water pipe had broken and flooded the barn floor, the dogs had been eating a dead white Leghorn and had feathers on their mouths, a raccoon had killed five hens and there never had been any 1080 on the place, I said, "See, things are never as bad as they seem."

"Oh, I don't know," Don said. "Bertha had 14 pigs last night and she has already eaten or squashed 12."

Awhile back we bought a 2000-acre cattle ranch in California. There are rolling hills, huge oaks and a view that encompasses two valleys, the ocean, and mountains. With the ranch we acquired 222 Hereford cattle and 5 saddle horses. Mother says that she intends to be photographed as the oldest living American woman still voting on horseback. I can picture myself as I teach my grandchildren to ride. I have yet to learn myself, but a neighbor, a friend of the late Will Rogers, says he can teach me in two days.

As soon as Don and I bought the place, a friend (male) sent us a Kiplinger report predicting a black future for the cattle business. Somehow I think it's going to take more than beef prices to change my nature. I'm *that kind* of an optimist!

—*Betty MacDonald*

*A*ny woman who thinks she's smart enough to chase hogs is either a bride or plain dumb. A woman just isn't built for hog chasing— yet, in a pinch, I have to do it! There's no escape.

Years of being a farmer's wife have taught me some signs that precede moving hogs, sure as tadpoles come before frogs. If my husband makes grim efforts to appear cheerful at breakfast, I know there are hogs to be moved. A peck on the cheek and a comradely spank mean they *all* have to be moved.

I trudge Indian-fashion,
ten steps behind him,
toward the hog pens.

Sure enough—"Got some time?"—he asks. Rolling a wary eye, I mention yeast rolls to be mixed, milkers to be washed. "This'll take only a few minutes," he says.

I know I'm hooked. Soon, in jeans and flapping over-shoes, I trudge Indian-fashion, ten steps behind him, to-ward the hog pens. I'm trying with scant success to look only half as ornery as I feel.

He clambers over the plank fence ahead of me and says, "We'll put that bunch in that door"—nodding toward three pens and four hog house doors. "You let 'em out."

Not wanting to appear stupid, I start toward the gate of the pen he's looking at. "Not those!" he yells. "I want the batch that farrowed the last of March!"

Walking slowly, I scrutinize the row of too-human eyes peering at me from between the planks. I try to divine the hogs farrowed the last of March from those farrowed

March first. After two false starts, I open the only pen left. Now the fun begins.

The hogs in front of the gate won't budge; then, as if at a signal, they pour through the gate, all 35 at once, heading in all directions. "Head 'em off!" Husband shouts over his shoulder, tearing after one bunch at a fast sprint.

I throw my head back, clench my fists and, knees high, give chase. I'm still in pretty blamed good condition for a 47-year-old, I tell myself. I get my pigs turned and, trying not to wheeze, trot back to the man. Do I rate maybe a pat on the head? Not so. "You chased the only ones headed in the right direction," he says glumlike.

Instant blindness sets in among the hogs. They can't see the right door, or even the hog house. Suddenly one starts at a determined run toward the gate she just left. "Stop 'er!" Husband yells. "If she goes back, they all will!"

A hundred and fifty pounds of pork and I clash at the gate. We are about pound for pound; but except for an irritated grunt, the sow doesn't know she's hit anything. I'm sitting in a mire of hog manure—with a tromped-on foot and blood trickling down one arm.

Eyeing my adversary from her own level, I holler: "To heck with these stinkers!" Husband hollers back. "It was stinkin' hogs like these that paid for your walk-in linen closet! Grab a board and whack 'er a good one!"

The sow, who has backed into a corner, glares at me balefully, head down. I grab a board (with, oh, joy, a nail in it) and I sock it to her. "Not there," Husband wails, "you'll damage the pork!" (I'd like to embroider her ham with a rivet gun.)

The sow decides I need more exercise, so she shoots past me out the gate as if jet-propelled. Husband, with the aid of snow fencing, has corralled the other 34 hogs at the right door, and obviously he can't leave them. So, giving full throttle, I chase after the runaway. She stops, turns, walks sedately to the hog house and into the right door....

Smelling more like those hogs than their own mothers do, I limp toward the house, the Medi-quik and a change of clothes. "Thanks, that wasn't bad, was it?" my husband calls after me. Feebly I wave back. It could have been worse; I could have broken a leg.

I am aware that, for our earthly consumption and profit, hogs are a necessary evil. However, when ultimately I cross the Great Divide, there hadn't better be a pig in sight. There will be no hogs in my little patch of heaven!

— *Ethelyn Pearson*

I'm "tool stupid!" I cannot distinguish a ratchet wrench from its socket relatives, and I don't know a ball-peen hammer from one that doesn't. To me, pipe threaders, pliers and drill bits are merely instruments designed to lacerate, gouge, maim and mangle.

...never dreaming I'd be expected to help unplug a straw spreader on a combine.

My patient, long-suffering husband was born with a set of silver screw drivers in mouth and he uses them with the grace and dexterity of an orchestra conductor. He can dismantle and reassemble a tractor during a total eclipse, and he labors under the false assumption that his wife is similarly endowed.

I took four years of home economics, majored in Baked Alaskas, and never dreamed I'd someday be expected to help unplug a straw spreader on a combine.

That man whose name I adopted just cannot understand my laxity in things mechanical, and the fact that I cannot successfully operate a tractor befuddles him.

Never once has he seated me on one of the roaring monsters in an uncluttered field with nothing to avoid but the horizon. But he'll order me atop a tractor with a very dead battery, throw a log chain over the whole sorry mess and proceed to drag me around the farm.

While his tractor snorts and bellows like a furious dragon, mine coughs in severe asthmatic distress and we busily dodge fence posts, flower beds, corn cribs, cats and trees. The dogs are yelping at my wheels in panic. Meanwhile, under my breath, I'm singing a quavery little tune, "This is the clutch, this is the brake. . ."

The real clincher came a few years ago; my ego is still smarting. I was asked to ride along on the drag (harrow) to give it "additional weight." His very words. "Why don't you refuse to help him?" my neighbor sympathized, when she caught me sniffling over my coffee cup.

"But he needs me!" I protested.

"Ha!" she snorted, "Did he need you the day you parted his hair with the file? Or the afternoon you backed over his foot? How about the time you turned on the electric fence just as he was stepping across? Or when. . ."

—Loraine Wallace

*W*hen we remodeled our kitchen we made it efficient so that I could finish my work and get away from that area. But my husband John still likes the kitchen and has added some touches of his own to it.

He moved the dining table from its out-of-the-way corner to the center of the room. "It's better for visiting over coffee," he says—and he likes to invite folks in for coffee. (He even makes the coffee sometimes.) In the corner he set a day bed with pillows where he rests.

Of course, that meant squeezing space for the radio—to catch the noon markets. Next, the TV and reading material appeared.

My husband has a well-equipped farm shop, but he may wash an air filter from the tractor in my sink (and if I'm not looking, dry it with a dish towel). While John is in the kitchen he catches me up on the latest farm news and samples whatever I'm cooking.

What a far cry from my planned kitchen. But I realize now that I have a kitchen filled with love and companionship. Why did I ever want to escape a room like that?

—*Leona Cwicig*

FALL

Who will rake the autumn
*   leaves*
And heap them in a pile?
I know who will do it.
I'll!

Mae Deck Hiatt

*M*y husband's grandmother was Scotch-Irish, but they say she closely resembled Queen Victoria. She must have also acted a good bit like Her Imperial Majesty; her favorite injunction to the grandchildren was "Bounce!"—meaning "Do as I say, right now!"

A lot of husbands are like that. (A lot more would like to be.) If yours decides on impulse that the two of you are going to Timbuktu *(and step on it!),* better drop your mop and grab your hat. That's a lesson I learned from my mother while I was growing up.

It was during those years that one of our friends divorced her husband on grounds of incompatibility. Their biggest wrangle was over what he called "the waiting game." She was a demon housekeeper who could never

Let the dishes stand, Mama. This is the best time in the garden.

turn her back on work. He liked to take the family tripping on a moment's notice. Mother was on his side. "There are things more important than housework," she'd say. "Things like good conversation, reading, picnics."

Papa's hobby was gardening. He would often holler for Mama to drop everything and put her weight on a lever to help move a boulder in the rock garden; or maybe she must stop and admire the plants he had imported from Switzerland.

One of my most satisfying memories is of hearing Papa say, after supper, "Let the dishes stand awhile, Mama. This is the best time in the garden." For over 50 years she followed him out into the sunset, well knowing that the dishes would wait until she got back. Not that our impractical father would remember to offer help!

Mama's reward? The most valuable one that a wife could wish for—the reward of being loved and needed all the years of her life.

A martyr begrudges every concession she makes, and too often wears a look of resignation. But a happy wife looks her youngest and loveliest when she goes along with some spur-of-the-moment idea produced by that man she married.

—Dorothy Albaugh

*W*hen a woman has to spend time in the hospital—and in traction, mind you—she has plenty of time to feel neglected. In my case (a slipped disc), all I could think of while being pulled limb from limb was that my husband hadn't sent any flowers.

Twice a day would come his worried phone call: "Can I bring you anything, honey? Is there anything you want?" I had only to say the word, but what woman will come right out and say "Yes, I want just one little posy." Flowers are something you can't ask for. They have to come unsolicited if they're to have any morale value.

And to make matters worse, my roommate in this city hospital was a lady foreman who belonged to things. She had impressive bouquets arriving daily—from the factory benefit society, her bowling team and card club.

Our window, which was on my side of the room, began

to look like a Say It With Flowers ad. Lying there immobile, in traction, with all those flowers beside me, I felt as if I were at my own wake. Without *one darn petunia of my own!*

Now my husband really is the most thoughtful of men. Twice he brought me a spiced-beef sandwich with my favorite pickles. During visiting hours he exhausted himself massaging my tractioned legs. (I didn't see the lady foreman getting that kind of attention!)

With all those flowers beside me, I felt as if I were at my own wake. Without one darn petunia of my own.

But he didn't catch on to what I really yearned for—not even when wandering patients would stick their heads in the doorway and exclaim, *"Look* at those flowers!"

"They belong to *both* of us," my roommate would say brightly, when the umpteenth bouquet arrived from her 47 girls at the factory. "We share everything, don't we?" She was determined that I shouldn't feel left out.

The time I caught her looking at me strangely over an armful of outsize chrysanthemums, I bit savagely into my spiced-beef sandwich with what I hoped was complete nonchalance.

Now, really, I told myself. Anyone can send flowers. But a spiced-beef sandwich takes the thoughtfulness and male obtuseness of your very own well-meaning idiot of a husband, who's been married to you 15 years without realizing that what you *really* want is a romantic something like flowers.

Finally came the day. . . . I went home, tenderly escorted by my mate. Then, completely disregarding the precarious state of my disc, for which I'd been strung on pulleys for weeks, I fell into the nearest chair and burst into tears. In my weakened state I broke down and made a clean breast of my unfulfilled hankering. "Not even one d-d-darn petunia!" I howled.

My poor husband was dumbfounded. Shocked. Flabbergasted. Sending me flowers had just never occurred to him. Besides, the room had been *loaded* with flowers. And I wasn't having a baby or anything, for heaven's sake—only a slipped disc!

"But so help me," he said, "if it ever happens again, I'll move in three redwood trees! With my bare hands!"

And first thing you knew, *I* was feeling sorry for *him!* But this experience taught him a lesson that all husbands might well heed—flowers make a woman feel cherished.

Now, come Valentine's Day, Easter, Christmas, my birthday and assorted anniversaries, I need not ask for whom the doorbell tolls—it tolls for me. And there, nestled among the lilies, violets or asters, I'm sure to find a single symbolic petunia.

—*Marion Benasutti*

WHAT'S IN A NAME?

HE called it just a common weed—
"Wild Carrot" with its wayward
    seed—
SHE put it in a lovely vase
And gently called it, "Queen Anne's
    Lace."

Lenore Eversole Fisher

The Beginning Years
SEARCH FOR FULFILLMENT

My Thoughts

All of us sometimes have great thoughts and
profound ideas which scud across our minds
like clouds across a summer sky. But most of
us don't take time to ponder through, and so
our inspirations are lost in the rush of spring
cleaning, or working in the garden, or in
the thousand things which occupy a farm
woman's waking moments.

In each wise comment by some great man
or woman, I recognize a brain throb of my
own. I thrill with a sort of parental pride to
discover that someone else has had my
thought; has nurtured and polished it, and
launched it for all the world to view and
admire. Thank God for people like Robert
Frost, Aristotle, Benjamin Franklin,
Thoreau, who have redeemed my thoughts
from mediocrity and made them immortal.

Genevieve Knudtson

*I*n the course of my life as a truck farmer's wife, I frequently drive a load of potatoes to the Cleveland markets. During these pre-dawn hours I mull over the multi-faceted life of a woman on the farm. Why is it that for some of us it is fulfillment rich and rewarding, while for others it is a wistfulness just short of satisfaction? I have decided a woman finds life rewarding only when she accepts her role and looks for ways to make something fine of it.

I think of an incident which occurred one morning. I sat on a crate at the basket factory, waiting for a truckload of bean baskets and scribbling on my writing tablet.

"Whatcha doin' there?" asked one of the workmen.

"Oh, I'm working on an article," I said.

Pondering that, he replied, "It don't make sense . . . a truck driver writin' an article."

Almost every woman harbors a wish to do something creative.

He had noticed a paradox in which I delight: Life can be full of an unglamorous hodgepodge of tasks, but that need not dull our awareness or stifle the creations which add meaning and joy to our days. (Behind the wheel of a truck I am Thoreau; some friends say my driving looks like it!)

My kind of creation is writing. I want so much to help others find fulfillment, as I have found it, in the raw material of an average life. I want them to feel the enthusiasm I feel for farm life in all its guises. I want to share the clump of bluettes which bloom with beauty—and courage—on my ill-nourished hillside. I want people to know what it is to ride a potato planter in the warm winds of late spring in air so perfect that you don't know where it ends and you begin. I want my readers to eavesdrop with me on the children's backseat conversation (what a diagnostic test of what you've put across).

Almost every woman harbors a wish to do something creative—paint, carve, garden, cook, write or pursue any of the dozens of crafts that let you express yourself. There is another sort of creativity—the talent for living a life which inspires others. I'm thinking of a neighbor who sells me eggs, supplying joy with every dozen. Her persistent optimism, appreciation of living and deep concern for each life that touches hers add up to creation as valid as the composition of a symphony.

It matters little whether we write or paint or transmit our enthusiasm to young girls in a 4-H Club, but *it matters terribly that we welcome life, not just endure it.* Otherwise, we lapse into apathy and boredom, then into self-pity. Enthusiasm for life—what a blessing.

One quality most necessary to a creative life of *doing* or *being* is encouragement from those around us. Encouragement is a genius we can all give, too—a kind of creativity in itself. For example, women who aspire to be creative cooks get over the urge in a hurry when each new dish is greeted with "Yuck! What's that?" Most good cooks, I've observed, have husbands who are patient with experiments and generous in their praise—and their children learn to follow suit.

No life can be creative which isn't constantly open to the enrichment of new experience. Every day outdoors can be a refreshment . . . the seasons in transition, a ballet of birds in flight. . . .

People, too, are an experience, each person teaching life in a unique way. Each day with a child is a marvel: When a 4-year-old asks, "What do ya' mean when ya' have peace?" he provokes profound thought. And each new child is a recapitulation of one's own life experience. Sit on a too small chair at the back of your child's classroom and you will rediscover the student you once were.

My husband Paul and I add constantly to our prized "people collection." We have a friend in a village in Afghanistan, a 6-year-old "son" in an inner-city ghetto, a friend in a Ghana mission, friends in city skyscrapers, farm friends in Europe. All add dimension to our lives.

Being interested in people may lead you to travel; you will find you can sacrifice almost anything for the price of a plane ticket. We have a threadbare carpet and burdensome mortgage payments like most other farm couples, but we rejoice in the memory of a winter trip to Europe when we were young enough to climb mountains and ski (we still are). A glorious trip in your thirties is worth three in your sixties. You can profit from the experience so much longer that it justifies an extra year of mortgage.

A day or two away from home—how do you get that freedom?

Reading and study are a way of life for the creative individual. Those who keep up with the news through magazines, newspapers, TV and radio tap a rich source of zest which costs little.

Finishing high school belatedly, getting a college degree or doing graduate work is much more possible for farm women today . . . and even more rewarding for a mature woman than for a girl. But degrees in themselves have little to do with enriching life—learning does.

Creative living demands that we see ourselves and our circumstances through other people's eyes. Our Danish Farm Youth Exchangee made keen observations about the shortcomings of American family life; coming early in our marriage, this was vital revelation—helpful. Visits to homes of friends allow our family to make discoveries—about the friends, about ourselves and our farm life.

I discovered the beauty of my home farm from a dormitory room in the heart of a city. When the trees began to leaf my freshman year, I was dumbstruck with the memory of all the country springs I'd lived through but never experienced. Spring on the farm has been a celebration for me ever since.

A woman who detaches herself occasionally from her husband and family gains valuable perspective on them and learns much about herself. One of the nourishing rituals of my life is an annual retreat for church women where I meet stimulating people and live richly and deeply for three days. There I discover a different me, one who broadens the viewpoint of the farm-wife me. Enrichment opportunities of this sort are open to women everywhere in this nation . . . adult education courses in high schools, College Week for Women . . . It takes inquiry and judgment to know the good opportunities; there is nothing so disappointing as a conference of many words, few ideas.

Creativity flourishes best in an atmosphere of freedom, where a woman is not plagued with unreasonable demands, inflexible schedules and rigid patterns of thought. Knowing all there is to be done, most of us farm wives are inclined to say, "Forget it." With four kids and an egg route, a Sunday School class and a demanding husband, what's freedom? A little time for private interests, for books, for entertaining friends and writing to them, a day or two away from home—how do you get that freedom?

There *is* no time if you are a perfect housekeeper. There is no room in your life for people if your household refuses to be crowded or off schedule; if disorder brings panic. Flexibility is the best answer I know (unless you're a super being. I am not).

You must have your family with you. My husband is

most willing to help me in my projects when I sacrifice time to help him with his. But I can take a pencil and clipboard anywhere; cuddled in my husband's quilted underwear, I sit against a fence writing between farm jobs. I may not look like it, but I am a liberated spirit.

Paul, in return, gives of his time and talents to rescue me from chaos in the house.

This kind of cooperation doesn't happen all at once, and there's grumbling from time to time; but if you bake bread, you can "jolly" a man into almost anything.

Many women could do more with their lives if they would trade certain of their responsibilities with other women. Independence ("I can do it myself!") is sometimes overrated; it can foster loneliness and frustration. There are nearly always women who will help—with meals, with children—if you ask them. But you must be willing to return the favor, even when it may not be convenient. To me, this interdependence is part of creative living in Christian community.

A woman who aspires to be creative is usually considered "different"; she must have the courage to accept this judgment. (For me, part of the charm of writing is to be regarded as an individual, unique.)

The end product of a creative life, whether tangible or intangible, shows the influence of all one's experience. Perhaps it is a home decorated in good taste or a meal showing flair with food. It may be just an average life out of which a woman brings a spark to warm and inspire others. For me, it is the tingle I get from expressing precisely what I feel deeply and yearn to share.

But the creativity most rewarding of all is keeping a husband encouraged and inspirited, stimulating your children, recognizing your own life as worthwhile. In this way a farm woman justifies the rare privilege of living on the land; and her creativity expresses her gratitude for the gift of life itself.

—*Patricia Penton Leimbach*

*S*o much is expected of a woman these days that you may have come to expect too much of yourself. You have several full-time jobs rolled into one, and they seem to be multiplying all the time. You're a wife, mother, partner in the farm business, community caretaker and, lately, some of you have become wage earners, too.

To make your life really complex, your roles often compete with each other for your time, energy and support: Should you go with your husband to a herd dispersal sale or to the PTA committee meeting? Should you work on those neglected farm accounts? Or squeeze out some extra time for Jim who has been suffering just lately from a case of teen-age mulishness?

To feel competent, a woman
must consider herself "somebody."

Choices like these weary and frustrate many women. Others manage to be all these things, but their satisfactions are tainted by the fear that they may devote time to one role at the expense of another. Then how do you keep from "tearing yourself apart"?

Well, first it helps if you recognize that all these roles are womanly and within feminine capabilities. You have to make your decisions and selections *on the basis of practicalities*—your time, your health, the needs of your husband, the ages of your children, but also *on the basis of your greatest satisfactions*. You have to decide about what you leave undone. If you feel satisfaction in one job has to be paid for by feeling guilty over something you don't manage to get done, your immaturity is showing.

It takes a mature woman who can "'see life whole" to accept that her time and energy are limited—and to feel right about what she does choose to get done.

You aren't your best self *if you live only for your husband and/or only for your children*. That's carrying the wife and mother business too far, because first you are *you*, a person. It's unhealthy, emotionally speaking, to "live for" someone else besides yourself. I'll grant that one way a woman finds her "wholeness" or complete personality is by giving to and doing for others. It's your nature. But only if you have a comfortable acceptance of yourself can you have a wholesome attitude toward your family and the world at large. Your own healthy self-interest is good for your husband. A man needs a mate with gumption and ideas of her own. And the way to rear well-rounded boys and girls who are "whole human beings" is to be one.

As a woman you have a chance to observe the self—a unique personality—born in a child, to give it freedom to grow, to give it the proper climate. There is a push within every baby to unfold and fulfill itself in the image God and Nature intended. Nourished by, loved by a whole woman, a baby grows this self-identity.

Read, study and grow—that keeps making your best self better. Education and training have become necessary to a woman's fulfillment. Knowing how to earn your way—whether you ever need to or not—satisfies your yearning for individuality. And today a woman isn't adequately prepared for life if she can't, if need be, support herself and her family.

I wonder whether we really learn anything by asking: Is a mother's work outside the home detrimental to her husband and family? It depends—what's destructive to some benefits others. Conflict over it is what's most disturbing—the indecisiveness, tension and guilt. (When widowhood or other calamity forces Mom to work she suffers no conflict and gets no criticism.)

Women today need to have purpose and feel valuable. A sense of worth and purpose may come more easily to farm women than to urban, because you have a central role in the family business which is intertwined in a close family life. Your growing interest in—and knowledge of—management problems of the farm business go hand in hand with your being consulted.

To feel competent, a woman must consider herself "somebody." How does a woman get this sense of identity and worth as a unique creature? The answer is: We are born with a feeling of "selfness" and can nourish it. Fortunately we can achieve it even if we've muffed opportunities so far. That's what education is all about . . . to learn and to grow as a person. That's what philosophy and religion are about—to give new dimension to your *self*.

—Dr. Aaron L. Rutledge

IT'S GOOD TO FINISH SOMETHING

As every woman knows, it is hard to remain serene when you feel frustrated over work that won't stay finished. Over the years I've found that serenity comes to me when I take time to create something—a visible something which won't have to be done over tomorrow or next week. My husband and children are proud of the things I make. They don't fret if I neglect routine chores a bit so that I can work on something I'm engrossed in. Like the big crocheted wool rugs I made for the living room and our bedroom, or the heavy sweaters I knitted for everyone in the family last winter.

Donna Warnick

65

*I*t is subject to many definitions, but I believe that creativity is this: the power to use all the growth we gain through our awareness of God's creation, and achieve something new from our own being—some new beauty, or realization, or tangible work.

Creativity! There is a word more talked about than understood.

Creativity is richness to share. Spiritual poverty comes when one fails to give of his time, of his abilities, of himself. The extent to which a person shares creativity affects him above and beyond influencing his material success. How fortunate that this priceless gift is not limited to those having great talents! Just about everyone is potentially creative—you, I, and the children we nurture. Our creativity begins, I believe, with our natural human heritage—wonder.

Observe the wonderment of a small child as he concentrates on a dew-spangled web in the grass or gazes at a train roaring by. That wonder—a curiosity *plus* about everything in the world—is probably your youngster's most valuable endowment for living. It is also a most perishable possession. Don't let your child's wonder dwindle and die! Cherish it and share in it. Help him question and examine and ponder and discover, until awareness becomes his essential way—an inseparable part of him.

If you have retained some of your own childhood wonder, you are your child's natural partner. But if you liter-

66

ally can't recall being bedazzled by something lovely or intricate or mysterious . . . well, at least you are not alone!

Why not campaign to win back what you have lost? The magic of wonder. . . . You might start by just not taking this evening's sunset for granted. (Every sunset is different—a once-in-a-lifetime miracle.) Or borrow this strategy of an Indiana mother—a *Farm Journal* reader:

"We have window breaks instead of coffee breaks at our house. The 4-year-old, her little brother and I have an enchanted window in the kitchen. Through it we read many a colorful picture story.

"We observe life's continuity—from rows of new green against brown earth in the spring, to skeleton stalks after corn picking is through.

"Such 'human relations' as we see among the wild life! Not long ago we saw a covey of quail bobbing along the edge of the cornfield. They crossed the road, and when they arrived at the green edge of the wheat, they formed two lines and started to dance! In, out, around. . . . Perhaps they were courting? We must 'look that up.' "

As she opens doors to awareness, this mother readies her children to build from what they learn—to become creators.

How can you be sure your children will be creative? Each child has some gift or special strength to use in the world and for the world. Since his use of that gift will be his unique expression of life, you can best help by seeing that he experiences life richly in ways like these:

Help him have quiet times at all ages of his growing—so he can listen, observe, absorb, reflect. This takes management in a big, noisy family! But even the smallest tyke needs some stillness in order to become acquainted with his world. The fragrance of mincemeat cooking. . . . The feel of Daddy's whiskers, of silverware, tree bark and pain. Sounds of wind sighing, flames crackling, piano notes rippling from a Chopin record. The taste of toast and of tears.

He needs time to see and to contemplate: leaf tones, falling snow, rain weeping down the window's glass cheek.

Help him know himself in relation to the world that's "so full of a number of things." In our school we play a game we call "Who am I?" and today the subject revolved around color preferences. Mary Beth decided, "I am a person who likes yellow." Why? "Because yellow is the color of the sun." And then—still analyzing: "My brother calls me Sheep Dog because my hair is long."

Help him express himself. Your animated conversation with Timmy about the tree house he wants may end up with his introducing the subject at school. That's what happened today in one class. Quick as a wink, the whole second grade was talking about tree houses, drawing and coloring tree houses and writing about them.

In Creative Writing, before we develop a subject on paper, we spend time hashing it over. I ask questions; soon the children start to weigh, challenge, debate and come up with "for instance." We also read what's been written on the subject—by great wordsmiths from Carl Sandburg to Walt Kelly, creator of Pogo.

We treasure-hunt for words—action words preferred. Tractors jiggle, joggle, rumble, roar. . . .Word games like that do help a child become amazingly fluent.

Be available to your children. From the strong materials of wonder, love and encouragement you help youngsters build a priceless power—to see beyond the obvious, to evaluate and compare, and then to create. This is the power that will give wholeness to your children and release their unique gifts to a needful world.

—*Sister M. Bernarda Sharkey, O.S.B.*

*N*early every child has at least one unique strength or talent. Only a few stand out, head and shoulders above the rest, in school work. But academic brilliance is only one kind of gift. Schools focus on it, but we mustn't let that blind us to children's many other gifts. We must nurture every gift of every child. Not to do this is sheer waste.

Peter has the gift of curiosity. Most youngsters merely do their assignments, take routine learning for granted. Not Pete! He itches to know everything about everything. The whole world fascinates him. His school work suffers sometimes, because he doesn't limit his curiosity to the assignment. His mind is always ranging, reaching; this is his special strength.

To make a good world, we need the gifts each child has.

And there's Bill—he's not gifted in the school's special sense; his grades are only a little above average. But Bill has another way of shining. *He has a way with people.* People like him. They like to talk with him, they like to work with him, they turn to him. It is hard to know what Bill's secret is. He is easy-going, is interested in other people. All this adds up to some miracle ingredient, and Bill has it to overflowing.

Bill's mother has a right to feel he is gifted. She has noticed and encouraged his gift since he was five. Talent with people is sorely needed in a world where skill in human relations lags far behind the "brilliant" skills of science and technology.

Elaine's also a dramatic example. No school would ever

call her gifted; but fortunately, her mother feels that she is. Elaine just passes in her school work; sometimes she is a little below average. But she works to get her grades. *Perseverance* is her rare and valuable gift. She will always be one who never gives up.

School grades are important. But they can trap us into thinking that they are the measure of all gifts. This simply is not so. Youngsters have many talents that aren't caught in school tests and that don't show up in grades. Let's look at Tom, a *B* student whose grades merely say he's "above average." Yet Tom is talented, for he has the gift of *ambition*. He sets his sights high. He uses every ounce of his power; nothing goes to waste. This means that all his life he'll do better than many who have more native intellect.

Joel's gift is *organization*. He's the one who engineers the games at the home room party. He's a top-notch administrator in the making.

I watched a 6-year-old boy the other day. Quite accidentally, a playmate hit him with a baseball bat—a glancing blow, but it hurt. The hurt boy walked away, sat down awhile, then he walked again. His eyes were swimming, his face was distorted with pain; but never once did he cry. There, I believe, was a youngster with the gift of *courage*. More than most children his age, he could "take it." We need people who have high courage; but we have no place on the report card to mark this quality with an *A;* so it may go unobserved and undeveloped, and another gift is lost to the world.

There is the gift of *coordination*—notice Jan's grace as she walks, runs, dances. . . . *Dexterity*—how delicately Mark works with a tiny screwdriver or fine wires.

Some children are gifted in music, in art, in dramatics. But don't discount the child who isn't; he may have another gift just as important. Alex can lift more, push harder and throw farther than the other boys. He can shove and lug and haul, and get things done better. His gift is *physical strength*. Don't ever minimize the importance of that.

Carol has the gift of *fluency*. She talks well, she is poised. Ruth, a quiet child, has the gift of *listening*. Cy's gift is *wit*—he translates it into clever cartoons.

Frances' gift is *perceptual awareness*. She appreciates beauty; she is sensitive to harmony, color, good design. Betsy is gifted with *energy*—you can't wear her out. George's talent is *calmness*—a soft, gentle patience that never fails.

To make a good world, we need the gifts each person has. I know a man who has the gift of *anger*. The rest of us may go along with unfairness or injustice, but he blows his stack! Thank heavens no one has ever squelched his fire. He keeps us from accepting peace at any price.

Another friend's priceless gift is a *sense of humor.* He is no clown, but time after time I have seen him save a difficult situation. When a meeting becomes tense, when tempers are rising, when anger alone is about to take over, you can count on this man. He's ready with the right word to bring on the laugh that breaks the tension and lets reason flow again.

Gifted adults were once gifted children—the lucky ones whose particular talents were detected and valued by parents and teachers. Look at what your child does. Look at all he does, with his mind, his body, his feelings; with ideas, materials and people. Don't pressure him! And do be honest—you don't help your child by seeing a talent that doesn't exist.

Once you take a look at the whole of him, you'll see an area where he excels. Having discovered his strength, you're entitled to feel good about it. Don't hide your pride and contentment. They are the necessary nourishment by which your child's gift will flower.

—James L. Hymes, Jr., ED.D.
Professor of Education, University of Maryland

71

The Beginning Years
CHILDREN

Growing Up

Raising a little boy is a quicksilver thing;
Restraint to him is a thorn that wounds his pride.
His arms are made for climbing, not to cling—
He will not walk on a surface where he can slide.
Tenderness cannot touch him through the day;
Let him be cowboy, Indian, what he will.
Think not that reasoning will make him stay
Ever in one place to be thoughtful, still.
He is a savage, spending all his strength
On wild and senseless schemes; but when the light
Measures a shadowed tree's elusive length,
Some magic unexplained destroys his might,
And knobby knees and elbows half retreat
Into a baby softness, transient, fleet.

Eleanor Alletta Chaffee

Dear Editor:

You've asked me, "Just how should you raise a boy?"

I'll match your brevity: "First, pick for him, as I did, the best mother in the world."

Any answer beyond that is too tough for an *amateur* parent. (And is there any other kind?) But, as one amateur parent to thousands of others, I shall rise to the bait, and cite what few ideas Mabel and I have found helpful.

See that each child has chores to do daily, but permit him to choose those chores, in consultation with Dad. This develops both decision and responsibility.

Our children (four boys, one girl) have quite agreeably picked their own chores. Harold (9) and Arthur (15) prefer to milk. Edwin (15) enjoys the sheep and lambs. Robert (12), our mechanical man, beats the others to the field, or drives the feed trucks for Tom, the hired man. Eleanor (6) helps Mamma in devious and doubtful ways, when she is not being bedeviled or adored by her brothers.

When social obligations get in the way, the chores are done early, or the boys swap around after some dickering. But never, never are they skipped.

Chores are done without pay. We consider them a contribution to the family for running expenses.

But garden work, tractor and field work in handling a farm of 525 acres, hauling manure and other man-sized jobs, are paid by an hourly wage, and always by check. The boys prove honorable in keeping their own labor record, and frugal in depositing that check.

Believe me, the incentive wage is not yet out of date. It's as American as hot dogs, and as universal as rest rooms. Mabel and I believe that a youth (or man) who gives full measure for his hire has already made third base and is sliding into home plate.

From previous years' earnings, our boys have already bought two pony brood-mares, two sows and litters, and six bred ewes for club projects. They aim to build up bank accounts for college.

Simultaneously, Mabel's wise guidance has steered them into giving much more than their expected tithe to our church—hers, like Mary's, is the "better part."

Mellow and heart-warming was the gesture by Harold who came to me with 25 cents, and this manly proposition: "You did my work last night when I went with Mama to the dentist. I figure it's about a quarter's worth." Of course I kept the quarter—man to man, you know—but I swear it smells of those very roses that my mother, now gone, used to mention:

*"Long, long be my heart with
  such memories filled,
Like the vase in which roses
  have once been distilled;
You may break, you may shatter
  the vase, if you will,
But the scent of the roses will
  cling 'round it still."*

Besides field work, operating tractors, and caring for much stock, the children are busy in youth affairs of the church and school, piano lessons, band, orchestra, and 4-H.

But even 4-H and church can overwork a conscientious guy. There's a lurking danger in overloading with both work and activities young and willing shoulders. That's why we've got the ponies, and have created the park and dam, with fish and boat, the ballfield—plus friends invited in to share them.

Three acres are in picnic area, but their yield in fun and memories is a bumper one. The hundreds of trees (Dad's labor of love) may not be too profitable, since they cost a little money, time, and tender care, with the Thomas grafted walnuts already bearing, the filberts, Chinese chestnuts, butternuts and Juneberries coming on, but these—aw, skip it: you editors wouldn't understand!

When we take a major business trip, one or another of our boys is sure to go along. Nothing novel about this, but, believe me, it gives you a chance to know your children as individuals.

At 10, Robert went along by train—sleeper, diner *et al*— to Denver; Arthur and Edwin have gone to St. Paul on cattle-buying trips. All the boys have made several trips to Omaha. (Sometimes they even miss school to go.)

Recently, Arthur accompanied me to Chicago, and in our absence, Edwin (Arthur's twin) looked after some 140 lambing ewes, with the help of my good hired man, who in turn handled the feeding of over 200 cattle and 200 hogs with proven dependability.

Incidentally, he and the boys are real friends, and help each other for no more reward than that of being helpful to someone you love.

Tucking that one boy in the car or train when you go on a cattle-buying trip can result in some rich hours of swapping stories, ambitions and secrets, and narrows down that barrier of relentless years. And further, the business ethics and tactics observed may well abide a lifetime, and can never be learned from books or from conversation.

Family trips are a joy, because Mama and Eleanor can go along. But I strongly advise that each parent make some special journey with each child. And don't wait too long!

Our pond and ponies draw kids from the village like bees to a blossom. To some parents, this could become annoying—depends on whether you call them boys or brats. A few have fallen into the pond. Three boys were kicked clear over a fence when they tried to ride the right pony in the wrong way.

But never have we discovered a really bad boy. And some of these visiting lads who fish for bullheads just might become President some day—qualifications in the recent past haven't been *too* high.

Grown folks, too, seem to like coming here. Radiant and inspiring are the Cunninghams, Ray and Ethel—YMCA leaders from Iowa State—who join us every Christmas season to share our joys and our children. (Their boys, Glenn and Wayne, used my horses years ago, were both killed in World War II.)

Ray tells me, as we fish or ride or hunt with my boys: "If this happens to you, you can be sure that the memory of these homespun joys will rise to bless and comfort and to make this glorious now part of a grand forever."

Our goals are these: that every child shall learn the challenge—and the reward—of work and responsibility; and (my own goal) that they shall share alike among them the duty—and the joy—of being kind to Mama in her twilight years; that they early learn to seek, and to find reflected in the placid waters of some quiet pool, the image of one's better self; and that they learn to bear disappointment without bitterness.

And so we hope that our own four sons may carry off to work, or to war, or wherever, a pocketful of memories that may sustain and inspire.

Any annoyance by visiting boys who cut up grafted apple trees to make wiener sticks is quickly tempered by recalling the words of Him who chided the scholars: "Forbid them not, for of such is the Kingdom."

Sincerely,
Clarence S. Hill

*W*hat is "Two"? Age two, I mean. It's all that is delightful and exasperating rolled into—Two!

Two is the most. He can hug the tightest, yell the loudest, spill milk the splashiest.

Two is a king. Look at him atop a trailer of corn, with the sun making a crown of his straw-gold hair. Anyone can see from his regal young expression that the world (our farm) is his domain. Sometimes the king is a demanding tyrant. When he's hungry, you feed him immediately or he will yelp. When he's "all foo" dinner, he must go to the bathroom now, or you'll change his pants and wipe up his puddles. Two must have every boat with him in the bathtub—all nine of them. And every stuffed animal lined up alongside him in his crib.

Two is the most. He can hug the tightest, yell the loudest, spill milk the quickest and splashiest.

Two is a gay blade, eager to rescue you from the boredom of dishes and dusting. Turn on the record player and dance—where'll you find a more irresistible partner? Swing your Two up, whirl him around. His peals of laughter are more important than housework.

Two is a food faddist. His meat must be dunked in his apple sauce; his bacon sprinkled over his cereal. Grapefruit looks prettier with catsup on it; even prettier with milk dumped over grapefruit and catsup. Two is a pest, in fact. Especially in the car, when everyone's dressed up for church. . . . Two's feet suddenly seem Size 13 as he tromps on Daddy's navy blue coattail, walks wrinkles in Mother's silk lap, climbs over in back to wreck Sister's black suedes and Brother's fresh shine.

Or, you're sewing today? Two will have the scissors, measuring tape, a piece of dress material (the left sleeve, probably) and your box of pins. You're watching TV? Two is determined to be a gunman, and you're his victim. If you don't "fall dead," he can shout bang bang 150 times more without drawing breath. If you do fall dead, he is pleased; so you must die 150 times more.

And Two is talented. He can wad his crib sheet into a lump faster than you can say "nap time." He then goes to sleep on a cold, plastic-encased mattress—head pillowed on Toby the Teddy Bear, legs poking out through the crib railing.

You pick him up gently, lay him on the big bed while you straighten out the gosh-awful mess he's made. As you return him to his crib, you notice—again—that his mouth is pure innocence, his skin is warmer and smoother and softer than anything else in the world.

You reflect that he is Two; that Two is exhausting, exasperating, delightful—and fleeting. That every moment of it is yours, to cherish and remember.

—*Elizabeth L. Boehm*

SO BIG

I collected mittens, sweater, snow pants, hooded parka, face mask and scarf for my 3-year-old to wear outdoors in the snow. He looked up at me and said, "But Mama, I don't have enough body for all that."

Janice Spieker

79

I have a hunch that there are real similarities between growing a child and growing a crop of corn or tomatoes. People who raise living things on the farm seem naturally to rely on the same kind of wisdom it takes to be a successful parent.

Successful child-rearing does not depend so much on book knowledge, or on specific techniques, as on your whole point of view—how you feel inside. I believe that farm parents have a very special chance to acquire the right kind of viewpoint. You aren't so likely to go against nature with children, any more than you would with crops.

You aren't so likely to make the serious mistake many mothers and fathers make with their youngsters: They are constantly rushing the seasons! They are not content with the natural order of development. They yearn for the blossom when only the bud is ready.

Farmers live by the natural order. I've heard them say: "It's too cold to plant." Or "It's still too wet to plow." Or "It's too early to harvest." A farmer has to have patience. He can neither plant nor harvest any old day he feels like it. The time must be right.

Timing also is the heart of bringing up children. Whatever you wish to teach them, the time must be right. The child has to grow; he must develop body power. His organs must grow. His muscles must grow. His whole nervous system has to mature. Psychologists have a word for the state when a child finally has grown enough to be able to learn. They call it *readiness*. Readiness means that the time has come—now the child has grown enough for the teaching to take hold.

If you try to teach your child any lesson at all before he is ready, you have no end of trouble—just as you have headaches if you try to plant a crop before the ground is ready. But so many parents can't wait. Their impatience is one of the big reasons for the battles they have with their children over toilet training, table manners, keeping clean, caring for possessions, sitting still, sharing, not interrupting. . . .

These accomplishments usually present no trouble if the child is ready. Trouble comes when you can't wait.

One way to build calmness and the good, easy-going patience you need with children is to realize: *There never is any waste season when nothing can be done.* Children always are ready for something, just as there is always important and worthwhile work to do, year-round, on the farm. There are fences to fix, machines to repair—and there's something you can be doing for your youngsters. Some parents seem able to think only of the eventual results they want. They want their child to get into college twelve far-off years from now. They want him to be attractive, well-groomed and well-spoken, eight years from now. They cannot be content with the youngster they have this very moment. They can't make the most of what this child can do now; they are too frantic worrying about his future.

---

*There are real similarities
between growing a child
and growing a crop of corn or
wheat or tomatoes.*

Every season is important. If a child can't walk yet, maybe he can crawl; and the more he crawls, the better. This is what he is ready for now. Or, if he can't crawl yet, he can go out in his carriage. The more he goes out and sees people, and hears sounds, and is stimulated by smells and noises and sights, the better. The baby is ready for this kind of learning, just as the ground is ready at some time to be plowed, harrowed or fertilized. Planting time and harvest time will come later.

To be a good parent you need to concentrate gladly on the job at hand. And you need to feel confident that a tomorrow always comes, with new tasks and greater progress. The need for this acceptance of today and confidence in tomorrow is especially strong if you are the parent of a 5- or 6-year-old. For example, so many parents worry about their small child's reading. They just can't wait. They must teach him to read; they push the school to teach him.

Most 5-year-olds and many 6-year-olds simply have not grown enough to be able to learn to read. But they love being read to! They love to go places and see things with their own two eyes. Take them to the airport, bus depot or railroad station; to the store or post office. They have grown up enough to look and ask and touch and smell. They come home full of new knowledge—more than most people could get from a book.

Or help these young children to do what they like best of all—make believe! Play-pretend is right for them now. They play fireman, policeman, truck driver, pilot, doctor, father, mother, new baby. . . . And all the while they play, they are practicing their language, stretching out their attention spans, stirring up their imaginations, learning.

Play brings wonderful growth to a young child. But so many parents can't enjoy the blossoming; they spend their time worrying over "how the corn crop will turn out." Confident farmers say "The crop is coming along fine," when at that moment the corn is only knee-high. With children, as with crops, it doesn't pay to have eyes only for tomorrow. You feel disappointed and let down, even when you have every right to be content. It all goes back to being able to feel a bit humble and realize the nature of growth. You can't make things happen exactly when and how you want them to happen.

I see this with the plants and bushes around our house. If I dig up a bush and put it where I want it, and that is all I think about—where *I* want it—the bush may die. Perhaps my place has too much sunshine or not enough. The same is true of children. You have to work with them. You have to keep your eyes open for what makes them flourish and what withers them or dries them up.

You have to respect children's interests. What a child does persistently, time and time again, has significance. The things he constantly turns to—or what he always rejects—are the important signals. You cannot see inside your child to know exactly how much his organs and muscles and nervous system have grown. The surest way of getting at his inside growth is to watch his behavior— what he thoroughly and fully gives himself to is what he is ready for.

A child's deep interest in something is the best signal you can get that he's ready to learn about it. You can help him, right now; but not by fixing your eyes on his far future, not by comparing him with the neighbor's precocious 5-year-old, and not by looking in the rule book for what to expect just when.

Watch your child, see what he seeks, respect what he reaches for—the way you respect all growth. If you help him this way, he'll grow well today—and he'll do well tomorrow.

—James L. Hymes, Jr., ED.D.

I want my son to grow up on a farm. Some will say that it would limit his opportunities. They may even feel sorry for him. But how can they know what his life and pleasures will be?

They do not realize that my boy will never be lonely; that Nature will be his companion for life.

I want my son to grow up on a farm.

Through Nature he will know that there is a God; that science does *not* control everything. He will learn to work hard and to be ambitious; but he will also learn to accept things as they come—the hail and the drought and the unforeseen.

As a farm boy he will know animals as good friends. In feeding and caring for those friends, my boy will learn the joy of doing for others. Early in life he will know a father's feeling toward those who depend on him.

To him all living things will be sacred. He will watch life appear and reproduce itself. He will learn the certainty of death. Its quiet presence in the plants and animals will assure him that life's end need not be feared.

He may find an Indian arrowhead behind the plow, and his wonder will kindle a love of history. A small animal's skull or a fossilized leaf imprinted on a rock will move his curiosity. Learning will be spontaneous, an adventure.

My boy will learn compassion. He will never forget the killdeer's nest in the pasture, and the fence he built to keep the cows from trampling it.

One of his pleasures will be a shack in the woods, where he will learn to love the stillness of a country night.

He will notice that each year the saplings around his

shack grow bigger. Then a day comes when he and his father cut the grown trees into firewood for winter.

He will realize then, that he himself has grown year by year, and that the time is near for him to start his life's work as a young man.

I want my boy to hear country church bells as he finishes his Sunday morning chores. The bells will ring again as he sits in church before the services begin. He will set his watch by the bells—they will help him chart his life.

I want the soil, the trees, the killdeers, the farm animals and crops, the bells of a country church, to be a part of my son's life.

He may leave the farm some day to begin another way of life. But his faith, his sense of duty toward others, his compassion—these truths that the farm has taught him—will go with him.

As long as he lives, there will be a little bit of the country in him.

—*Karl Ohm*

*S*pring vacation turned out to be the best week in 12-year-old Orrin's year. He put in 40 hours of work painting for his uncle, and he hurried his lunch so that he could spend that hour learning to weld. Notes appeared by Dad's alarm clock: "Wake Mom and me up early." Even then he pre-empted the call, eager to be up and off to his job.

"Child labor!" Well, you could call it that. It was really adult labor produced eagerly by a child.

This was not Orrin's first job, of course. The boys started loading small bags of potatoes when they were 4 or 5 years old, building pride along with strong bodies. At 7 or 8 they spread fertilizer with a tractor and spreader. By 10 and 11 they could load their own spreader from 50-pound sacks, having spent several years working gradually through 10- and 20-pound potato sacks.

They learned to handle tractors on their parents' laps, starting with very slow pickup work in the harvest season and working up to the fitting and plowing. By the time he was 10 years old Teddy could back a four-wheeled wagon up an incline into a narrow barn door, a feat that can often leave a grown man frustrated and swearing.

They did the other small jobs required of kids—the lawn mowing and the household chores. They did (and do) them as reluctantly as all kids, with prodding and threats and shouting and tears. What they hungered after were the challenging things the adults were doing, and so gradually we entrusted these things to them.

We have come to realize that when entrusted with adult responsibility, youngsters produce like adults. There are few farmers who wouldn't rather trust their equipment to their early teen-age children than to adult hired help. The difference is the lifelong conditioning, the observation and concentration that a farm child invests in a task long before he performs it. Nobody teaches a farm boy to drive. He learns it by "osmosis."

Surely it's a hazardous business and everyone looking on is critical. But we always felt that a child who guided a tractor down a row in low gear at age 5 and learned very gradually through the years stood a better chance of being a safe operator than one who was sent out to fit a field for the first time at 12 or 13. (No cards and letters please. In our situation it was right; in many others, it may not be.)

It is not, however, this responsibility beyond his years that gave Orrin such a thrill with his spring holiday job, though surely that is what prepared him to perform the job more eagerly than any man. It was the memory of tedious days spent on his knees picking green beans for 40¢ a basket. That is valuable conditioning that you cannot buy! As I tell all of my little bean pickers year after endless year, when you have submitted to the discipline of bean picking for a summer or two, every other job you perform will seem easy. "You have nowhere to go from this job but up!"

If a child's first job is picking beans, he learns the discipline of hard work. From then on, other jobs are easy.

Soon my phone will begin to ring and small voices—kids of 11, 12, 13 or 14—will ask if they can have a job this summer. If they tell me they're 16, I say, "Sorry, you're too old for this job." By the time a kid is 16, it's too late to make a bean picker of him. He has already learned that he can make more money for less work at almost anything. But if he starts at 11 and earns $1.50 a morning he has really accomplished something. If he sticks at it for three or four years, you can bet your bottom dollar that he'll never be on the welfare rolls and he'll probably move into the high income scale.

Paul, my husband, picks alongside them sometimes to increase the challenge and demonstrate what's possible. But I am the labor foreman. The kids say I wouldn't last two days at General Motors—too strict! Wherever farm or business leaders get together they complain about the lack of good help. We don't. From the best of his bean pickers Paul chooses his hourly work crew, and he'll proudly match them for work output against any group of $5- and $10-an-hour adults.

Paul is proud of his potatoes and his green beans, his corn and his melons. But the finest product he produces year in and year out is good workers—dozens of them every year—for the labor market.

"Child labor!" It has a nasty ring left over from the sweat shops of the Industrial Revolution. America's children have been carefully insulated against the "cruelty of hard labor." But I haven't met the kid on whom you can inflict hard labor!

The notion that young children cannot, should not, need not do meaningful work for at least a couple hours every day is a ridiculous one. When I recognize the great value my sons place on their few free hours I think that we must be the luckiest people alive. I have spent days and weeks and months in school "study" halls riding herd on children who were suffering from an insidious boredom, and were far more difficult to manage than my sweating bean pickers.

As for Orrin, he's hoping that he so impressed his uncle with his prowess as a painter and a welder that he'll never have to face another bean field as long as he lives.

—*Patricia Penton Leimbach*

*I*n the late fifties, parents who were still resisting TV were in trouble with their kids. Our four grade school children felt underprivileged because we didn't have a set. TV's all the other kids talk about, they claimed.

My wife and I really pondered if we were doing the right thing in holding out. We didn't want our children to feel branded as different, but neither did we feel compelled to let what the neighbors did, and our children's whims, dictate our family life. (When that happens, children sometimes go through life expecting the world to be handed to them on a silver platter.)

We drew up a bill of rights for parents.

Of course we were pleased that our youngsters' friends like to come to our house because we *do* things—not just watch TV. But the situation raised the question in our minds: Can we live pretty much as we'd like? Or should we, like many parents I've known in my years of work in the field of family living, simply resign ourselves to taking second place to the children until they are grown?

We finally decided that parents should be allowed some privileges, too. So we drew up a Bill of Rights for parents, just to remind ourselves not to let our lives be completely submerged in the interests and activities of our youngsters. Here are the "rights" we feel entitled to:

1. We have a right to make rules. Certain boundaries, wisely set, help a child learn to live with limits. "We don't play ball in the house" is not a subject for debate.

Too many limits, though, keep a child from learning to

think for himself. A student told us that he didn't realize until coming to college that a boy could consider spending any money without asking Dad. It had never been done that way in his family.

2. We have a right to be different from other parents. When our children want to do something, they use the most lenient parents in the neighborhood as an example to show how strict we are. Even the kids wouldn't want us to be like those families in all respects; so we don't try to live by other parents' standards.

But the right to be different doesn't mean we disregard entirely what other families are doing. The "uniform" for the fifth grade is blue jeans—for boys *or* girls. We go along with this undressed-upness rather than have the kids picking fights just because "I was so dressed up to-day I couldn't play scooter tag." We know that a child who consistently has to be greatly different from his friends will find the going rough, and may rebel.

3. We have a right to make parental mistakes. Children are marvelously resilient—they bounce right back after misunderstandings—so long as they know you love them unreservedly. In fact, some rough places can help toughen them for living in a world that's far from smooth. But we try to learn from mistakes, and do better.

4. We have the right to disagree with our youngsters, so long as we let them disagree with us. And if we listen to their ideas with respect.

Differences in taste, opinion and ideas are normal and good. Once we got TV, we disagreed (like other families) on which programs to watch. We let the children sample almost everything, but give our reasons for preferring some programs.

We think the children must develop a sense of values in order to cope with the confusions of a lifetime. We can help by letting them see what we stand *against*—and what we stand *for*.

5. We have a right to show our feelings—but we must see that the children take our feelings in stride.

It's no use to pretend that everything is always sweetness and light. You can't hide tension and anger, and if you only *half*-hide them, the children will sense something is wrong and magnify it. Better for ours to hear me grousing about my trying day than to *feel* my mood and think they're the cause.

But we do try to exercise self-control. The children would be seriously damaged and learn little about adult ways if I went around kicking the cat on days when everything goes wrong.

6. We have a right to privacy. Parents, as well as children, need some time to themselves—to read, to think, to do as they please. We respect our daughter's diary and our son's desk drawers as off-bounds; they respect our occasional closed door—and we all keep hands off each other's mail.

7. We have a right to be worried. Every newspaper and news broadcast bring us anxieties about the world, our country, our town. We're also concerned when the kids don't get along rapidly on the piano. We try to remember not to waste our worry-energy on things we can't (or shouldn't) do anything about. But being concerned about a state of affairs can point the way to a constructive remedy—so we don't worry about "worrying" our children sometimes.

8. We have a right to seek help. Today professional people are spending their lives studying problems of childhood, parenthood and family life. Families gain insight through study clubs, guided reading and adult education. We don't feel we're losing face to admit that we don't know all the answers; we're grateful when someone else can help us.

9. We have a right to our friends. We recognize the need

for our children to have friends, to share mutual interests, pleasures and concerns. It's just as important for us. We take time for neighboring.

10. We have a right to continue growing, as persons. We try not to become so absorbed in being parents that we lose our own identity. After child rearing has ended, how empty life will be if we've let the children become our sole reason for living.

Although our family is our first interest, the world has much to offer beyond the walls of our home—and our family life is enriched by outside interests. We continue to square dance—and my wife and I don't feel guilty if we take a vacation for two.

So that's our Parents' Bill of Rights. We think every family should have one. Yours may be different from ours and still be good and workable—for yourselves and for the grown-up people your children become.

—William M. Smith, Jr.
Professor of Family Relationships
Pennsylvania State University

PRAISE YE

As the earth drinks rain
After parching days
And responds to the sun's
Beneficient rays
So does a child
Blossom forth under praise.

May Richstone

I'll never forget the day I discovered the rewards of letting a trifle remain a trifle. We were to meet some friends at the airport. The youngsters—scrubbed, dressed and combed—waited for me in the kitchen. I entered the room just in time to see a carton of milk hit the floor.

My 6-year-old stood in the middle of the widening white puddle, milk flowing down her dress and onto her shoes. Her brother had escaped the deluge; but both looked at me fearfully, waiting for the storm to break.

They nearly got it, too—the tirade they expected. If ever I wanted to break into angry oratory, it was at that moment! But, just in time, my sense of humor came to the rescue and I said just three words: "Get the cat."

The children laughed, I laughed, the cat lapped. In this fairly relaxed state we changed Sally's clothes and departed—only a *little* late.

Unwittingly I had happened upon a large truth: When things go wrong, quiet acceptance, tempered with lively humor, is the *easy* way out for a parent! Children usually don't mean to cause trouble—things just happen. But a grownup's anger can scare a youngster, or make him resentful, so he'll go ahead and make a bad matter worse. It's a lucky parent who learns to accept a mishap for what it is—a trifle.

And how lucky is that parent's child! Such a youngster can say "I'm sorry"—and mean it—without losing face. He can also learn, the *easy* way, to recognize trifles himself—and not build them into tragedies.

—*Alys McColl*

I wasn't trying to disrupt the livestock sales yard. I simply was trying to help my high-school son get a picture of his FFA pigs. But the man galloping by me on horseback shouted as if he thought me deaf as well as a little dumb: "Lady, get out of the alley, or you're going to get hurt!"

Another voice bawled over the loud speaker: "Thirteen head! Alley one! Pen eighteen!"

I grabbed my purse, camera, and the Future Farmer's small brother, and started to scram. "You can't leave now!" someone yelled. "They're coming down the alley!"

Just in time, we shinnied up the fence. Thirteen head of wild-eyed steers raced by, their horns fanning my ankles.

We made three other attempts to get out of the way; but each time, a bunch of cattle was hustled toward us, and we had to seek the fence top again. I gave vent to my exasperation by screeching at my 5-year-old: "So help me, if you ever join FFA or 4-H, don't you expect any help from me!"

I didn't mean it, for of course he will join. And so will the Future Farmer's other younger brother. And I shall remain knee-deep in baby chicks, vegetables, fat steers, and bottle-fed lambs—all those many projects necessary to the making of a boy into a man.

One comforting thought is that the ordeal certainly is making a woman out of me.

Show me the boy who has earned merit badges, medals, blue ribbons, or a trip to a national meet—or, for that matter, a boy who hasn't won anything, but who is ready to try again next year—and usually I can show you a mother who *should* look like a five-star general, with a chest full of ribbons.

But Mom's ribbons and badges are not so tangible. They are the pride she wears (right there on her sleeve) in the accomplishments of her boy; and her own realization

94

that it's as necessary for her to help, and direct, and encourage that boy, as it is for her to feed him and make him wash behind the ears.

Sometimes I wish I were the woman whose chief concern when Fair time rolls around is to get Grandma's vinegar cruet entered in the antique section. And sometimes I envy the unharassed poise of my city friends who can stroll past the exhibits, innocently assuming that chickens' combs always shine, and that steers' tails are naturally curly.

"So help me, if you ever join FFA or 4-H, don't you expect any help from me!"

But I am a little bit sorry for them, too. They've missed the biggest part of the show, known only to those who enter by the back gates armed with buckets and brushes. We are legion—we who have coddled half-dead lambs by the kitchen stove, or helped hold a steer while Dad and the boys clipped his "whiskers."

I have taken many projects in my stride in the course of our son's 4-H and FFA career. Scouting, too. I have mastered the Morse code, and I have taken the Five-Mile Hike and eaten aromatic stew out of a can. We—Dad and I—have applauded our son's victories, and helped him starch his spine to stand up to defeat. But often I have wished that I had never met Doris.

Perhaps, subconciously, I feel inferior to Doris because of her pedigree. My ancestry is a conglomeration of nationalities; but Doris's is untainted by any intermingling of blood lines except the best Spotted Poland China.

She wasn't a very impressive pig the day she made her

debut in our family, kicking and squealing against the sides of the spud sack in which she was carried. But as of today, she has a fistful of ribbons—Junior Grand Champion, twice Grand Champion, Reserve Grand Champion— and I never can help feeling sort of apologetic as I give her garbage from our humble table.

Our life has not been simple, nor dull, since Doris entered it. For one thing, the will power of a mule is mild compared with that of a hog if she decides not to climb into a trailer. The only way *I* want to cope with that situation is to get behind her and whop her with a stick.

But Doris must not be struck, nor scolded, nor yelled at—it would make her nervous. She must be enticed with bits of apple, or lettuce chunks, or warm mash, held temptingly before her. Doris must be coaxed and cajoled, praised and patted, until getting into the trailer becomes her own idea.

She is even superior in the matter of progeny. In the past twenty years, I have managed to have three children: Doris celebrated her first birthday in the midst of eleven offspring.

Eight of the piglets survived their mother's pure awkwardness. They reached the 56-day weaning mark on one of the hottest days of early summer. This was the very day my son must get his litter-weight contest entry forms in the mail.

Weighing those pigs was a job for the family! I hope St. Peter was watching, and that he gave me credit above and beyond the call of duty; because helping swing 60 pounds of stink and squeal around on a sweltering afternoon is not a job I'd ever apply for.

By Fair time, Doris's litter had become about a ton of pork to load, and the pigs met us wth menacing grunts every time we approached them. But, once we got them to the exhibit, they made a fine showing. And, although I muttered "Good riddance," I felt a real twinge of regret while helping load Doris's family for its last ride—to become chops and bacon via the FFA sale.

I did not feel a part of the bustle and noise of that sales yard. Men were there, with strident voices, and they belonged. So did the boys and girls scrambling around the enclosures, giving final brushings and pattings to their animals. The white-shirted, cigar-smoking businessmen in the buyers' section belonged there—but not I. Nevertheless I wanted to see this thing through.

Then the bidding began, and I saw a girl weeping into the sleek neck of the steer just sold to the butcher. I saw a boy's face brighten until it glowed incandescently as, quarter by quarter, the price mounted on his fat lambs.

I listened as, again and again, the bidding on all the animals climbed—*Going once, going twice . . . SOLD to the Bank and Trust . . . SOLD to F. W. Woolworth Company . . . SOLD to Barlow Warehouse!*

What profit, I wondered, is there in a businessman's paying more than the market price for a pig or calf?

The realization flooded over me that herein lies the profit: This is the American way of showing that our young people are our priceless possession. This is our way of saying to them: "It isn't easy to be young, to learn good sportsmanship and good business practices—whether you win *or lose*. But we believe in you, and we want to help."

And suddenly I was proud to be a part of it. Sometimes it's nerve-racking, fatiguing, and downright inconvenient to be the unsung helper behind the scenes of my son's projects. But it's also tremendously rewarding—a manly son is blue ribbon enough for any Mom!

—*Eleanor N. Fowler*

The Striving Years

HOW DOES A YOUNG WIFE MANAGE?

Dear Editor:

Last night I had company—a woman whom I like very much. But I couldn't be at ease. My house was a mess. That's so often how it is; I almost dread the sound of car wheels on our driveway. I work hard, day after day. But I have so little to show for my work that in spite of everything I feel I've failed.

Like so many young marrieds, we haven't much money and have few conveniences. My days are filled with my three little ones, the house, sewing, laundry. I do take time for my children so we can do things together. But even my husband remarks: "This house looks like you've been gone a month."

My morale gets lower each time some crisis points its finger at my shortcomings. I try to keep up the most important things; yet I can't get enough done. Constant interruptions get me so far behind that even baking a favorite pie assumes staggering proportions.

Out of the wealth of experience so many other farm women have had, can your readers give me pointers on how to manage with some degree of efficiency? I've wrestled with this problem alone year in and year out—without success so far. Now, I'm asking for help.

M.M.

*D*ear Mrs. M.M.
Reading your letter was like looking in a mirror.

I, too, am an "almost" type of housekeeper—almost through with the cleaning, almost finished ironing—almost dead.

Until I overhauled my viewpoint, I regarded housework as menial, monotonous, degrading. My eye was on the circumstance and not on the goal—to be a good wife and mother and have pride in this career I chose.

In a young mother's years of *doing* it's easy to get the false notion that hard work in itself is a virtue. (You may know women who make drudges of themselves with too much dig-dig, rub-a-dub and moppy-plop.) But in spite of good management, life's unexpecteds can knock perfectionist housekeepers off their well-dusted pedestals.

Ask yourself first: "Whom am I trying to help and please in this job?" My husband, myself and our children, in that order, I finally discovered. Not my perfectionist mother-in-law, my own indulgent mother, nor visitors— whether drop-in callers or lingering guests. Most overworked homemakers set their standards too high. So my advice is: Don't strive for perfection.

Yes, it's frustrating to be caught between a critical husband and several young master-mess-makers. When my own husband made the crack, "Looks like I'd better bring my shovel over from the barn and dig out," I answered: "Thank you, dear, for offering to help. Where shall we start?" That worked.

The two times my husband washed diapers made such an impression on him that he went out and bought a washer, money or no! We women like to be reassured over and over that our work is appreciated. So we value our spouse's moral support as much as his actual help.

When the house isn't up to snitch, the children and I try to give Dad a specially warm welcome so he notices us and not the clutter. (Too much chaos makes him homesick for his mother's neat-as-a-pin housekeeping.) But I think a husband needs a cheerful wife more than a perfectly kept house, for men resent their wives always being tired. I've read that resentment is the most tiring of all emotions. You can use up all your energy for a whole day in a few moments of rage. On the other hand, when your mind is at peace, your body can perform many tasks without fatigue. You're more likely to organize, not agonize.

A flexible plan, not an impossible one, is the best answer I've found to cope with "so-much-to-do, so-little-time." Let's face it, you can't really schedulize because your farm setting and your role of mother guarantee interruptions. The idea is to break those endless tasks into bite-size pieces, then work like sixty. Being productive, even for a short time, will give you a glow of competence. After accomplish-nothing days, tell yourself: "There's always tomorrow."

I list my jobs to be done in my reminder book under the headings: *Gotta, Oughta* and *Hope To*. If you don't assign jobs a priority in some way, you'll be tired before you're halfway through your list. One other bit of psychology I use on myself: I'm sure to include some jobs that give me special satisfaction. When I need a lift, I go outdoors. (Usually I feed the sheep, stopping long enough to burn papers and empty garbage.)

Don't put off the *Gottas* and *Oughtas*—putting off makes jobs harder since you suffer through them mentally and they still aren't done. Dread of a task is more tiring than the actual work itself. So things I dislike doing, I do as early in the day as possible. Makes the whole day go better.

Have you ever counted up the number of decisions you

make in a single day? They're enough to tire you—especially if you make them alone. But making up your mind about what to do and when to do it comes easier with experience. Deciding what's right or best in rearing the children often ties me in knots. When you can't avoid mistakes, learn to live with them peaceably.

It's monotony, not routine, that women dislike. And routine without frustration is a giant step toward efficiency. Here's an example: I can automatically take out of the refrigerator whatever I need for fixing breakfast, so I open the door only one time.

Whom are you trying to please? Your perfectionist mother-in-law?

I timed myself for several days once to see how long it took to do the dishes. Actually I found it was such a short time that my fuss about them was hardly worthwhile. And meantime, I speeded up the process. See if you can figure out the things you do the hard or wrong way and how you can improve. (Just now I'm struggling to dress our youngest quickly in a way that will foster more self-help on his part and less irritation on mine.)

But routine and habit are blessings since they free your mind to think. Fortunately, ideas aren't confined to an eight-hour day. Doing dishes is my time for contemplation. While your hands grade eggs, you can look ahead to how you're going to redecorate the living room. The next time you iron, first read something that really interests you. Then as you iron, ponder on what you've read. Doing two things at once is then your next easy step. I keep my sewing machine in the kitchen and do mending while I'm getting meals. Now I can watch a pot and stitch on a patch without spoiling either.

Making a job harder than necessary isn't smart. But sloppy housekeeping can produce accidents and tension, and tension is infectious—the whole family suffers. Children seem to behave better in an orderly house, and they learn to appreciate nice things by living among them. Besides, you'll find work easier in an attractive home.

Usually I operate on the principle that a good sweep is better than a poor scrub. But if one of the children is sick, or there's some other crisis, I resort to sensible slights: I may decide not to sweep *or* mop, and something about that conscious decision keeps me from feeling guilty about the neglect. And I'll have more to show for my time if I spend 15 minutes straightening the clutter of the day.

Young farm wives sometimes have to accept life without the icing in the early years. During our pre-washer days I used to say that the only thing automatic around here is the children—they're automatically hungry 20 times a day. But gradually I've accumulated some inexpensive labor savers I wouldn't do without: a laundry cart, an adjustable ironing board, a dry-and-steam iron which saves sprinkling, a minute timer, a vegetable peeler, a good can opener, and a supply of sponges for wiping up spills. (By this time I'm sure you've learned the truth of: "Children and plastic go together.")

If you can manage installments, keep getting one "servant" at a time. We've always felt the hours saved were worth the interest charge. With or without money, keep rearranging for greater convenience—especially kitchen and cleaning supplies—until the house begins to fit the needs of your family.

Children enjoy working with their mother as well as playing with her—they don't really know the difference if a job becomes a game. In my own king-size nursery the vacuum becomes a bulldozer. One youngster carries the cord and follows me, the driver, around the room. The tiniest climbs onto a chair where he won't get bulldozed and squeals with delight when we come in his direction. Toys can become lost gold to store in a treasure chest.

I never refuse anyone's help. Most of us have elderly relatives or neighbors with too much leisure. They like to mend, sew buttons, even peel peaches during canning time. They will love you making them feel needed again.

If your husband can help with your brood, so much the better. Sometimes we mothers are to blame for making fathers feel the children are our sole responsibility. Your husband will love you and the children more if he fills his role in the family.

With your mind at peace, you're more likely to organize, not agonize.

When you have good health, problems don't often assume staggering proportions. How long has it been since you had a complete physical check-up? Many young mothers feed their families properly, take them regularly to dentists and doctors, insist on naps—but neglect their own health. Even borderline anemia can sap your energy, slow you up and make you feel always behind. Working to the breaking point may appear heroic, but it's poor sense for you.

Take time to brew yourself a cup of tea and use the best china. That will help you feel more like an individual and less like a housekeeping, baby-tending machine with most screws loose.

The reflection in the bathroom mirror sometimes upsets us more than the eternal cycles of meals and laundry.

Think you can't be pretty while you clean house with 30 sticky fingers grabbing at you? How would you handle a dirty job in a factory full of attractive men? Even if you can't often enjoy a beauty shop hairdo or look picture-pretty at 11 a.m., you can manage a quick spruce-up before your husband comes in for meals.

Best remedy for frustration is to do something you enjoy—especially something creative. Enthusiasm actually tunes up your body to supply energy for doing things that give you pride and pleasure. And without time for something you like to do, you're likely to have a mental chip on your shoulder.

If you can trade baby-sitting, get away from the house and children occasionally. You need to talk to other grownups—sometimes I feel like a blithering idiot after a day of exclusively preschool conversation. During visit-while-we-mend sessions with friends, I've noticed that often we can solve others' problems better than our own. (Besides you may feel comforted if the house you visit is messier than the one you left!)

I'd recommend at least one outside interest that will keep you alive mentally. Above all, go out in the evenings with your husband as often as you can.

How can any woman feel she's failed when she counts the jobs she has—nurse, bookkeeper, cook, laundress, rocker of babies and comforter of all ages? I admire a mother who takes time to find out what's going on in the minds of her children.

Is there a mom who feels at the end of the day that her work is done? I never do. We need to learn to live with work undone—we'll always have some. But the outcome of your efforts will show best when the children have grown up. How they've matured, how they've learned to meet situations, how they've made their contributions to the world. Meanwhile you're giving them love—helping them to be responsible.

There will always be days when wheels in the drive will give you shudders. You'll sometimes despair at the family zero hour—between five and six when the children are hungry and cross, you're tired out, the house is a mess and your husband wonders what you've been doing all day. Then it's time to realize the value of being wanted and needed. Some day you'll probably look back on these as your happiest years—that's what some older women, now lonely and bored, frequently remind me.

Remember, too, you aren't wrestling with problems a-lone. Writing this, I feel such a kinship with you. I don't know whether you have dark hair or light, whether you have a tendency to overeat (as I do), what you like to read. But I love you, because you are me, and we are legion.

—*Many women's letters in one*
edited by Laura Lane

ashday brought me a wonderful gift, something of great value—a snail shell I picked up in the grass under the clothesline. As I held it in my hand, my mind searched out a verse of Scripture I had learned somewhere along the road of daily living: "He hath made every thing beautiful in His time."

Even a snail's little spiral house, I thought, turning aside from the basket of wet clothes so that I might see this shell in more detail. It was perfection—a house in complete order.

At length my wonder and admiration gave way to thoughts of my own house, at this time far from being like the shell in my hand, softly white and clean with orderly chambers. It was what we women call "a wreck." The sink held unwashed dishes we had used at breakfast and nearby was the washing machine waiting to be drained and cleaned and shoved away. And our Littlest had rushed off to catch her bus for school, leaving her bed unmade and her pajamas lying in soft little heap on the kitchen floor.

A snail shell taught me the difference between housekeeping and homemaking.

The men folk in my family had been litterbugs last night, and liked every moment of it. Their litter was still in the living room where bedtime had caught them— newspapers scattered on sofa, magazines on chairs, gun cleaning items on the table, and a record wherever a clear spot could be found to place one within handy reach of the record player. Underfoot in this same room are the Littlest's crayons and coloring book, her games and stuffed animals (the solitary places in a house are not for her).

Looking up from the shell in my hand, I wished that my house could be like it, white and clean with order in its chambers. An orderly house would be heaven on earth for me, something I could be proud of—instead of making apologies for—whenever company dropped in.

The wind swooshed gently through the locust trees. I took another look at the snail shell in my hand, thinking: I've seen all of it and now I'll slip it into my apron pocket and give it to Ann later for her nature collection. But it suddenly occured to me that nothing lived in this orderly shell! There was emptiness rather than orderliness. The disorder of my own home now began to have a new and satisfying meaning.

I slipped the shell into my apron pocket and thought joyfully: "He hath made every thing beautiful in His time." Even my old farmhouse with its uneven floor boards. Homes are to live in, and living leaves tangible bits of the family scattered throughout the "chambers" to give the rooms the warmth and joy of our life together.

—*Genevieve Tate*

*D*o you ever long for just one meal in peace; one dinner with no milk spilled and no arguments over the vegetables? Do you sometimes dream of a blissful future when nobody wakes you up in the middle of the night for a feeding, and when nobody ever wets his pants?

If you have such moments—if living with young children gets you down—let me tell you our story. You'd probably call it a success story. Because we can say honestly: They don't do it at our house anymore! Nobody has crayoned on a bedroom wall for ages, or used the scissors to mow her own hair, or made designs in lipstick on the sheets and pillowcases.

The living room furniture in our house stays put now. I can sit down in confidence, without looking. Nobody ever moves my chair over to the piano stool, and drags a spread off the bed to make a hideout.

Our home has a whole new air of dignity. When the guests arrive nobody bluntly asks: "Did you bring me anything?" Nobody wonders out loud: "Why are you so fat?" Pocketbooks are safe—nobody dumps the contents all over the floor. Eye glasses are safe; so are watches.

Can you figure out how we did it? How we got rid of the crises and hubbub of having little children in the house?

The youngsters themselves get most of the credit. *They grew.* They are school age now: in elementary school, junior high, senior high. They can do more and they can keep from doing more. Plain healthy growing up is a large part of this "success" story.

But we adults deserve credit, too. We tried to live right. We didn't crayon on walls. We liked milk and drank a lot of it. We wanted our hands to be clean. And we loved to sleep. Going to bed wasn't any punishment for us. We napped every legal chance we got.

As they grew, the poor youngsters were trapped. They couldn't help but "catch" some of our good behavior. Oh, we did enough reminding and insisting. But, looking back, I suspect we put in most of our good licks during the pleasant, happy times, not during crises.

A blissful future when nobody wakes you up in the middle of the night.

Yes, we've been "successful." Our house is tidier now, and much quieter; really very quiet for hours on end.

In fact, sometimes you could even call it lonely. The children are in school. They are out with their friends. They are taking lessons on something, somewhere with somebody. They are at a club meeting. . . . We adults, in our quiet house, have all the peace we can stand—a little too much at times.

Slowly the idea grows: There may be more to successful

child-raising than finally having a quiet, neat house. Maybe true success lies in enjoying children while you have them. You can call it "getting your money's worth" all along the line. Maybe you lose if you wait for the fun and appreciation to come through memory, ten years later when "they don't do it anymore." All those little childish "crimes"? The best answer may be: Let them die a nice slow natural death. You don't have to choke them out.

Right now our young basketball-crazy adolescent is aiming a tight-wadded paper ball at a metal wastepaper basket. Every time the wad goes in, the metal reverberates like a Chinese gong. And, hit or miss, every time 130 pounds leap and land, shaking the house.

Success? It comes from knowing that those are nice noises—the kind to enjoy *now*. They will be a lot dimmer, paler, feebler, when you hear them only in your memory.

—*James L. Hymes, Jr.*

*I*t was one of those nerve-jangling days. Our 4-year-old Mike pinned a clothespin on the dog's ear. The poor victim yelped and streaked through the screen door. The washer coughed up suds all over my freshly-scrubbed floor. And just when I was up to my wrists in pie dough, the phone rang. My husband was calling from a neighbor's: Would I take a broken hitch to town for repairs?

Several years ago I might have spanked the 4-year-old for playing tricks on the dog. I might have yanked the dial off the offending washer and raved that I'd trade the machine in. I might have told Vance what I thought about having to drop my work to run his errands.

Result: A miserable family and a tension headache.

Headaches really settled in when my husband had an accident with a field cutter and lay unconscious in the hospital for a month. Tranquilizers only sent me floating into space. So, while Vance recuperated, I did some down-to-earth thinking: There must be an easier way to cope with life's attacks on the nervous system!

Instead of an earthshaking scene, we had a calm talk.

First I had to accept the fact that I am not an easy-going, sleep-in-the-dentist's-chair person. Children's accidental food spills annoy me. Sudden shrill noises play tick-tacktoe up and down my spine. No mother can avoid these occupational hazards; but, I decided, any mother can make herself more shatterproof.

Since then, when a situation arises, I try to remember the saving formula STOP, LOOK, LISTEN—AND COUNT TO TEN. That day of the dog and clothespin incident, I stopped instead of grabbing the hairbrush. I looked and saw tears in my little boy's eyes. I listened and heard him sniffle, "Didn't mean to *hurt* Spot, Mommy!" And, as I counted to ten (figuratively), my reason asserted that our son hadn't been deliberately malicious—just curious, like any normal 4-year-old.

Instead of an earthshaking scene, we had a calm be-kind-to-animals talk. We examined the clothespin and discovered how hard it could pinch. Then a contrite Mike held the box of tacks while I repaired the torn screen, letting off steam constructively with a hammer.

Unfortunately not all problems and solutions fit into a

neat, quick pattern. Machines usually do what they are dialed; for example, the oven can ruin a cake at 550° when busy little fingers tamper with the range. (I've learned to keep a watchful eye on projects under way.)

There are plenty of places to pour bottled-up tension. While I polish silver to work off a black mood, my mind gradually ascends to more pleasant paths; the shine I put on our tea service is reflected in my spirits.

But household chores can themselves build up tension, can induce mental fatigue the same way homework affects a 12-year-old. I reward myself at the finish line. For instance, I allow a half-hour to read when the ironing is done. Creative self-expression—painting, writing, music, knitting—helps counteract demanding routine.

As heart of the home, a mother must maintain the steady beat of serene living. By cultivating calmness, I try to help our children build strength to cope. They'll need that, in a world already marked "highly explosive."

— *Mary Ann Gourley*

COMPLETE COMPLIMENT

It was our eldest son's night to do the dishes, and I had to be away. Upon returning, I complimented him on the good job he had done. No answer. Thinking he had not heard, I repeated it more loudly. From the other room came his reply, "I'm waiting for the except."

Pat Turner

*W*hen my husband Paul comes in from the fields and misses me, the children may tell him, "Mom's gone over the hill again." This means that things at home have become more than a trifle thick and I've walked out for a spell.

I would like to be the soul of graciousness and serenity, enjoying all my work. But I am not. I am impatient with weeds, I detest doing dishes and I can be blind to a dangling cobweb for a month. If I am also exasperated about the price of hogs, I may blow up simply because small Bill and his dog break a bucketful of eggs, or because the girls have been pokey with their chores today.

I leave the ironing, baking and gardening, and escape into the timber.

Suddenly I may recall an admonition of Scripture: ". . . provoke not your children to wrath." Then I know it's time to go over the hill.

Over the hill is where the Boy Britches come first in the spring, shooting up overnight. Little Bill picked huge fistfuls one April day, and Joan taught him to say "Happy Easter, Mommy" as he presented them to me. We had ham for dinner that Sunday, and Bill's wild flowers arranged on the table.

Over the hill is where fat old frogs gossip at our pond. Once our neighbors got a gallon of frog legs there in an hour; but our delight is in the frogs' antics, not their table value. Barbara, age 14, likes to toss a pebble in their midst and watch them leap up and plunge into the water.

My hill descends to a small brook that twists along to

join Big Creek. Big Creek is forbidden to the children, but here at the brook I see the dam the girls built last week. Beside it is the small corral of twigs Barb contrived to confine a young mole she captured. I've suspected Joan of tender skulduggery in connection with the mole's escape; she was that upset over Barb's plan to dissect him and study him under her microscope.

One hill leads to another. In season, that next slope has a pink and white carpet of Spring Beauty, and beyond that is a hill where we cannot walk in April without crushing blue blossoms. Bluebell Hill may soon be leveled to make a new highway. So we have a special duty. Every time one of us visits the timber, he digs up some bluebells and transplants them to the grove farther on.

Here is the hickory grove. I pat the dirt round my bluebell transplants, hoping our efforts to move a hillful of flowers will be successful. We must cut a branch of this green hickory; then at our next cookout we'll smoke up a storm in order to hickory-flavor our hot dogs.

I might as well go on to Big Creek and check the creek gaps. When water rises after a rain, debris may dash against the fence and cause a lot of damage. But all's well: in fact, some new patching on the barbed wire tells me that Neighbor Brown has been here before me. One unforgettable dry year, Mr. Brown offered to cut our mutual boundary wires so that our cattle could pasture on his land and drink from his spring-fed water hole there in the creek. Whenever I check the creek gaps, I remember that drouth and Mr. Brown's neighborliness.

Circling back toward home, I see a bunch of our Angus, black jewels against my hillside. The curious calves approach me, but the cows are skittish and I do not bother them. The May apples hang heavy beneath broad, umbrella-like leaves, and in the spring Sweet William and violets bloom at this spot.

Now I have come full circle, and here's home—needing

me, no doubt! The young ones rush to meet me. Little Bill flings himself against me exuberantly; Joan is talking a mile a minute; Barbara's eyes shine a quiet welcome.

These are my good kids; here are the home and farm I love. How could I have been so annoyed with them only a couple of hours ago?

"Where have you been?" my husband asks. I say, "Oh, just over the hill," and the grins we exchange mean we both know that everything is pretty much right again.

—*Myrtle Felkner*

WHITE SPACE

White space is what we editors call the area on our pages not taken up by type and pictures—it sets off what we have to say, just as space sets off the branches of a tree.

Empty space in your house will do the same for you. Every room needs some breathing space, free from pictures or patterns or objects. These restful areas of nothingness set off the things you do want your family and friends to see and enjoy.

Each day needs some "white space" as well—some mental breathing space, to set off the activity and give it meaning.

Gertrude Dieken

The Striving Years

FAMILY AND FARM

Investment

Until strange weeds we could not name
  were pulled from near the gate,
Until dead limbs were trimmed away
  from poplars, tall and straight,
Until a fence we had not built
  was gleaming white once more,
Until a purple clematis
  was climbing near our door,
Until, with tools shaped to our hands,
  through years of pleasant toil
  we'd planted yellow tulip bulbs
  in unfamiliar soil,
Until the scent of lilacs
  had invaded every room,
Until spring lambs had frolicked
  in an orchard pink with bloom,
Until we'd walked the furrows
  of each dark and fertile field,
Until we'd watched new crops mature
  and harvested their yield,
Until our shelves were stocked with jars
  of food that we had grown,
We'd merely bought a little farm . . .
  but now, we really OWN.

                     Lois Carpenter

I started dreaming of a sign on my big red barn, "Campbell & Sons" when my first boy was born. After all, working with your children is supposed to be one of the great joys of farming.

Well, I've had considerable experience with their enterprise by now, and I'm having doubts.

About the time Danny was eight, a heifer delivered premature twins in a ditch and died. The freezing calves were nearly gone, too. Being very busy at the time, I hauled the calves to the barn, laid them in some hay, and said to my son, "Save them, and you can have one."

"My calf is up and drank a quart of milk, but, too bad, Dad, your calf died."

When I came in that evening from the field, he raced to me. "My calf is up and drank a quart of milk," he told me proudly. "But, too bad, Dad. Your calf died."

My second son, Jack, was given two pet pigs to raise. I soon noticed his pigs were about twice as big as mine. He was giving them all the milk and supplements and feed they could eat, before feeding mine at all. "Put them with the herd," I instructed. "Feed them all together." "Sure, Dad," he cheerfully agreed.

Next time I was present at the feeding, his two pigs were serenely gulping milk in the middle of the trough. My forty pigs were trying to sip a little from the ends, their eyes cautiously on the switch Jack was waving warningly at them.

When my daughter, Donna, was ready to buy a calf, I told her how to choose a fine one, mentioning points like size, conformation and color. But when they drove a shaggy little Hereford into the sale ring, she clapped her hands and shrieked: "Look at the adorable pink nose! That's the one I want!"

She worked from dawn to dusk, with that one calf. It ate royally—the most expensive feeds in the local store, choice bits from my bales, lush, handpicked grass, roasting ears snitched from the garden, grazing from my alfalfa when I wasn't looking. A cattle feeder eventually paid a handsome price for the calf. As I grimly counted bills and figured I was only in the hole about seventy dollars on it, Donna joyfully deducted from her check a brush, bucket and ribbon she'd bought. "Oh Daddy, isn't farming great? Now I have enough money to buy four calves!"

Along came Mike, wanting to buy his own sow. He was too young, but he saved the money for her by denying himself treats at the store and rides at the summer fairs until we gave in. His sow decided to be a mother one stormy, zero night. He insisted on sitting up with her, so I had to be there, too. Ten o'clock, nothing; eleven, nothing. We told each other all the stories we knew, sang some songs, traced the family tree to all its branches and roots. Twelve o'clock, and one pig. By one o'clock it was clear to me that that was the crop, just one pig and he was dying. I didn't want Mike to have to face those hard facts at one in the morning. I carried him to bed.

My wife, hearing the news, insisted on getting up. We must go to the barn and try to save that pig. Too late. It was dead. As we reentered the house, a quivering, yet brave little voice from upstairs called: "How's my piggie?" "Things are fine, go to sleep," my wife answered.

Then to me she whispered, "You'll have to go to Elmer's and see if he will sell you a pig before Mike wakes up."

I agreed. We ought to get *something* out of that sow after all the feed she had eaten. So I slept two hours, got up and drove to Elmer's.

I came home with seven pigs and an empty wallet. About five, as I drank coffee, Mike came down the stairs, three steps at a time. "How many pigs have I got, Dad?"

"I haven't seen your sow yet this morning," I told him. I never lie to my kids. I hadn't seen her. In fact, I was so sleepy I couldn't see at all. He ran out, coattail flying, cap and overshoes forgotten. He came racing back, jumped the last six feet, and grabbed me, yelling a song of glee and triumph: "I've got seven! Seven! Oh, golly, seven! Gee, Dad, for awhile there, I didn't think I'd do so good."

Well, by then it didn't feel so bad, being broke.

I've about decided I'll just paint that sign "Sons & Campbell." They sure make more money than I do on these deals. They must be better businessmen.

—*Rex Campbell*

*G*etting rid of anything down on the farm these days is next to impossible. Everytime someone gets ready to do a good cleaning job in the house or barn, some purist comes around screaming, "Don't throw *that* away. They're paying fabulous prices for that stuff." Where, I ask, are all these people paying those "fabulous prices" for barn siding and Mason jars and old bottles, rusty nails, wavy window panes, hand-hewn beams, and—are you ready for this one—worn and faded blue denim?

Yup! I was just fixin' to go down in the cellar and take a clean sweep of those dusty old overall jackets I inherited with Nelson Newberry's barns. (When you buy a neighbor's farm, his fields and buildings traditionally carry his name ad infinitum.) And then I read it right there in *Time:* Saks Fifth Avenue is selling faded denim jackets for $26, and bikinis made of old denim go for $20. Wow! If Nelson Newberry thought his overall jackets might be resurrected as bikinis, he'd have himself reincarnated!

Bikinis made of old denim go for $20. Wow!

Odd as it seems, there's real justice in placing such value on genuinely faded blue denim. (It seems they try to simulate the faded effect, but imitations don't command the price of the real thing.) In order to achieve real "patina," blue denim needs to do a lot of bending in the sun and whipping in the wind. It needs to be dunked in farm ponds and ground into the slag of playgrounds. It needs to fall from horses or motorcycles or bicycles a few dozen times, and be forgotten on a fence post for a few weeks. It should kick around in a dusty pickup truck a while. Most of all it needs to be soaked repeatedly in sweat. It has to lie in dirty laundry piles on damp cellar floors and hang for long spells on clotheslines. It needs to be shortened and lengthened again and mildewed in mending piles and be nursed back to health with patches.

Then and only then does a garment of blue denim have real integrity. And believe me, it's worth more than any city slicker's money can pay.

I wonder idly, while I'm pondering the new values, if there's any market for a retread farmer's wife in her midforties who can bake bread in an old black stove, make apple butter in one of those old kettles, can tomatoes she raises herself in those old Mason jars, make butter in a stomp churn, and manufacture faded blue denim as a matter of course.

—*Patricia Penton Leimbach*

*S*ometimes, quizzes printed in the women's magazines let you rate yourself as a wife, but they don't apply to the predicaments we face on the farm. To fill the gap, I've designed a quiz for farmers' wives. How would you handle your husband in these farm situations?

A farm wife's kit of answers for any little crisis.

● *You're driving a full load of bales out to feed cattle; your husband is perched on top of the load. He hammers on the cab roof. You don't know what he wants, so you slam on the brakes. Fourteen bales and your husband soar into the air. Do you*
   (a) turn up the radio so you can't hear him
   (b) ask, "Is this where you wanted to unload?"
   (c) cry.

● *You're ready to leave for town when he reminds you that he needs cigarettes. "You'd better write it down," he says. Stung, you reply, "I can remember that!" But you don't remember. Do you*
   (a) drive 30 miles back to town
   (b) suggest he stop smoking
   (c) dig to the bottom of the freezer, where you put some supplies after the last time you forgot.

● *He stops by the house to pick up his lunch and asks if you'll shut off the jet pump in an hour. "Sure," you agree. Then you lay out the pattern for a new dress. Later that afternoon, you step out the back door into six inches of water. You*

(a) grab a hoe and start ditching

(b) do all the chores so no one will have to use the back door that evening

(c) say you soaked the yard especially well and want to plant grass.

- *In spite of hints, he forgot your birthday. You*
  (a) burn his egg
  (b) buy a neat pantsuit, hand him the bill
  (c) wait—he'll think of it eventually. Anyway, if you don't have a birthday, you don't get older.

- *You're rushed getting home and turn too fast into the lane. There are deep tracks where you came back out of the ditch. Do you*
  (a) hope he won't notice
  (b) tell him you swerved to avoid hitting a cat
  (c) get out the rake and smooth over the tracks.

- *He says, "I love you." Now, do you say*
  (a) doesn't everybody?
  (b) then how come. . .?
  (c) I love *you*.

If you picked (c) on the last question, the other answers won't matter much. But you might still want to keep this list handy for reference. A farm wife is bound to need a lot of answers!

— Wilma Shauers

I once kept track of the time my father, brother and I spent hunting grease guns, drawbar pins, jacks and wrenches. The total: I won't tell you, because you'd never believe it. And I'm not even counting seven woman-hours of help by Mother and various sisters; three hours by the gas man and two salesmen who helped hunt a funnel, a checkbook, and a fan belt; the vet, another half hour hunting a rope.

Dad generally starts the hunt.

"Who ran off with my . . . . ?"

"It didn't walk off, you know."

"I'm going to buy a lock and . . ."

There you have the symptoms of "who-took-itis" or "pliers-dropsy" or "wrench-amnesia," an inherited disease of males passed on from father to son with no symptoms on the female side.

Dad comes striding.
"Who ran off with my . . . ?"

No man ever believes he has it. My father will come striding across the barnyard, his face drawn. "Someone," he says solemnly, "stole the hitch off the mounted mower." We search. Dad says he left it along the road where many people must have seen it. The Stolen Theory begins to sound plausible. We assemble for a council of war.

Shall we or shall we not call the sheriff? My brother remembers the dogs barking through the night. One of the girls thinks she saw a car parked down there, or at least going "awful slow." The breadman says there've been robberies on the other side of the county. We wonder how a thief could get the blasted thing unbolted, especially at night, but we say nothing. We've found the villain. So we buy a new attachment. Weeks later when the "stolen" one is found, we agree it's good to have a spare.

Over the years we've tried cures. Dad once came home from town with half a dozen hammers. We stumbled over them in the barnyard, kicked them out of the way to get doors closed. No tractor seat or shop chair was safe to sit down on. It was a gloriously secure feeling. But by the end of the month, we were down to two. For awhile Mom had a tack hammer in her sewing box that went by the name of "Momshammer" and was used in emergency hammer shortages. Until, in one such emergency, Dad tried driving spikes with it.

During the boom days of the '40s, we expanded to five farms several miles apart, with several tractor outfits and sundry part-time hired help.

We lost wrenches, sure. We lost needle valves, spark plug wrenches and V-belts. We even lost track of a four-row cultivator and two 16-foot harrows!

We couldn't fritter away time on tools and equipment. There was always another 50 acres to plant or harvest, lurking somewhere over the next hill. Harrows dragged hastily into a woods at the end of spring planting, passed out of memory by wheat sowing time in the fall.

Once I tried to put 20 feet of electric fence—that I'd left strung along the edge of the wheat—through the combine. I shifted the fence over into the adjoining cornfield, and sure enough, Dad tried to run it through the corn picker in the fall.

There came a day when we all resolved to do better. No more tool dropping. No more litter. We even tackled the spot back of the barn where junk mutiplies like bacteria. We tore down all old buildings so that we could mow the whole farmstead clean.

It was beautiful.

But for only a week. Then someone dropped a stone

about six inches high in the center of that spotless sweep of ground. It seemed an innocent litte rock.

Three hours later there were two end wrenches lying on it and an oil can beside it. Shortly after, a 5-gallon gas can. By chore time next day, a grease gun, and an ax. By Sunday morning, a two-by-four, a half sack of fertilizer, a canvas, a calf bucket, a broken sickle, a battery and four cats. The pile was now big enough to put things behind it. After that there was no getting rid of it. In the fall we removed the pile completely, but by then it was too late. The habit of dropping things there was firmly entrenched in us, even though the rock was gone.

—*Gene Logsdon*

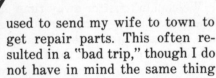used to send my wife to town to get repair parts. This often resulted in a "bad trip," though I do not have in mind the same thing the current drug culture talks about.

So I started writing down every little detail I could think of, like the age of the machine, whether the part was for the left side or the right—things like that. But I'd forget the apparent, and when my wife got to the dealer's counter, he'd listen to the description and then ask: "Is that the green or yellow one?"

I decided I'd have to train her. Next breakdown, we went out to the cultivator and looked it over first. I explained the function, position and shape of the thing. Then we went to town together.

"I need a new shank for my cultivator," I said airily.

The counterman opened up his huge tome of new parts and asked: "Is your serial number under or over 60,000?"

I gulped. A suppressed giggle behind me. "What's the difference?"

He brought out a couple of shanks. I decided the larger one was right. Charming wife said: "That's bigger than the one at home."

I'd have to train my wife to buy repair parts.

I graciously explained the difference and stressed how important it was to look the machinery over before leaving home. . . .

When I went back to town for the smaller shaft, I took the old one along. "This is what we should have done anyway," I explained to her.

After the next breakdown, she soloed into town with the old part.

She came back with one just like it, but informed me there was a newer model of that part, too, that would fit.

"You should have brought it. We should take advantage of improvements."

She remembered. Next time there was a choice, she brought the improved model. The older type cost $6; the new one $47.85.

I made myself a promise that day. It's worked out pretty well. We have a lot more togetherness as the two of us ride to town side by side.

—*H. R. Betzelberger*

I've always thought only farmers in our neck of the woods talked to animals and things.

Like my father. Without doubt, he's the most garrulous man alive . . . with things that couldn't possibly talk back.

"Go ahead and blow off, you stupid roof," he shouts at the tin-covered barn during storms.

And one of his favorites: "Bless you, bulk tank, you do keep a cold melon."

Naturally, one must eavesdrop to hear such talk. One thing Father cannot abide is being caught in the act.

"Bless you, bulk tank, you do keep a cold melon."

On the other hand, our neighbor Geeby Bewaldi (everyone thinks that's a made-up name) carries on conversations with his tractor outfit that can be heard 20 acres away—easy.

"Quit squeaking," he roars at the disk. "I just greased you an hour ago!"

Sometimes his threats dissolve into abject pleading.

"Don't run out of gas, now," he begs the tractor. "We've only got two more rounds to go."

Geeby becomes downright gabby when he's fixing something. Like when a burr is rusted to a nut and refuses to budge. "Well stay there then," he yells. "I didn't want you to come off anyhow." Then, to make sure the nut got the message, he whacks it with the wrench.

But I've found out that farmers are carrying on oneway conversations everywhere.

Once I worked for farmer in Minnesota who loved to

sing in the field, but he claimed that every time he did, something broke down. He almost convinced me, too. No more than five minutes after he'd start singing there'd be a loud "caroom!". . . followed by a big cloud of smoke and dust and a high-pitched burst of profanity.

Willy would stand back and glare at the offending machine. "Dammit, can't stand to hear me singing, can you? Just can't stand to see a man happy." He'd keep talking like that all the while he repaired the break. Willy was stubborn, but after a while you wouldn't hear much music out of him. I guess he came to an agreement with the machine. If it would work, he'd quit singing.

As I approached the barn of an Indiana friend, I overheard the following: "At least you could cooperate here in the barn . . . all you did all day was lay in the shade."

There was no one in the barn with my friend. Not a hired man, not a boy, no one. Yep, you guessed it. He'd been lecturing a cow.

Come to think of it, talking to creatures and inanimate objects may not be as safe as it used to be. *You have to be plenty careful what you say to a computer these days!*

Gene Logsdon

BIG JOBS

Big jobs I don't mind—like cleaning house and helping in the field. It's the little things I dread—like sewing on a button.

Lena Jeffries

*E*merson said, "The way of life is. . . by abandonment," but you can't kid me. The way of farm life today is by acquisition! One man quits or dies or moves to town, and his neighbor buys up the property. Every farmer knows the pattern, and every farmer's wife lives with it.

Paul always coveted the Schuster farm. "Best soil in the area," he would say. It is a mark of my insensitivity that I didn't know how deeply he felt it. But his father Leimbach had said the same thing of "the Schuster place," and so did his grandfather. In an era when land was cheap and tiling a field was something of an extravagance, some

---

Good land means more to farmers than almost anything else.

Schuster forebear had dug up the place and painstakingly drained it. The heroics of the effort were not lost on the Leimbachs. That was when the desire was planted that this year bore me painful fruit.

Paul never drove past the place in midsummer without appraising the abundance of the crops; and the covetousness of his remarks was ill-concealed. Farmers are a matter-of-fact lot. They don't rhapsodize about it, but good land means more to them than almost anything else. Paul really took spiritual possession of that place years ago.

When the three bachelors who owned it grew too old to farm, and put the acreage into soil bank, Paul chafed at the disuse of good cropland. It was painful for him to watch it finally grow up into thistles and yellow dock. He was prompt to respond to a request by an heir to come over and mow the place. I should have known then that he

130

wouldn't be happy until it was his own.

Farmers' wives, who are more inclined to measure wealth by fluid assets, don't get as carried away by this drive for land acquisitions. So when the property was finally offered for sale, I fought the purchase all the way.

"We already have more land than I've found time to walk over," I protested. "Don't you realize you're going to be 90 and 10 years dead when I finally get that property paid off?"

Paul had found himself an able ally in his farming partner, Ed. They sat down with their record books and Ed's little calculator and figured that they could make it.

"What are we going to do with another old house and all those barns?" I argued.

"We'll sell them; just keep the land. People are dying to get a little place in the country that they can fix up."

"The only way you could fix up that house is with a bulldozer!" I said. Might as well have saved my breath. The land instinct is deeper than reason with farmers.

They discussed the matter with the man at the P.C.A. office who shared their optimism. "You'll struggle for awhile, but in the end you'll make out." All they heard was the "make out." All I heard was the "struggle."

So we bought the Schuster place. Paul and Ed are as happy as birds. They go with their shovels and repair the drain tiles; they mow and trim and clear away rubbish. The day they put the "For Sale" sign on the farm house they had a veritable celebration.

I stay home and wring my hands and ponder ways to increase the income to meet payments. But life inflicts its irony upon hard-working men like Paul and Ed. I have a feeling born of long observation that in the end they will have the "struggle" and their widows will "make out."

—*Patricia Penton Leimbach*

*Y*ou're probably like me. Before I married into this business with built-in southern fried, the word "birds" meant something cute, like canaries. Well, my ex-baseball player sweetie is not the canary type. He means "broilers." And every ten weeks, to show just how much he means it, he plays mama, papa, psychoanalyst, and baby-sitter to 11,000 of the whitest, most prima donna bunch of feathered hypochondriacs ever to scratch litter on a lady's shoe.

That lady is me.

Being courted by a broiler grower is just as much fun as being courted by anyone else, except not too many other girls of my acquaintance get kissed between the broiler mash and the supplement. We got our handholding done, not at the movies, but while waiting to throw the switch to start the feeder tracks. And there were the times, too, when my Lothario wouldn't even show for an evening; then finally appearing, would say with a grin that he'd been sitting up with "sick friends."

Before I married a broiler grower, "birds" meant something cute, like canaries.

Those same "sick friends" at least stayed away from the wedding ceremony, although we did absent-mindedly carry a bag of grit all the way from Iowa to New Orleans. But even at that, they almost deprived me of a groom the day before the wedding; on his way home to see them, he skidded his car on the ice and threw a wheel.

While honeymooning in the South, other people visit the ante-bellum homes and Antoine's famous restaurant.

We visited the ante-bellum homes, Antoine's, and also every broiler house between Iowa and Bayou Plaquemine.

But after we'd settled into our little insurance-covered cottage, and I had learned to put my garbage into empty feed bags like the other chicken widows, a new phase developed. The disappearing acts began. Vacuum cleaner—electric fan—measuring spoons. "Oh, I borrowed it for the broiler house," my spouse would admit cheerfully. At least marrying me had taken the pressure off his mother who had lost three garden hoses and her best bread knife.

(And what do broilers do with vacuum cleaners and garden hoses? To be perfectly honest, they merely occasion the need, and believe me, they never need the occasion. Our richest by-product of the industry grows two-pound tomatoes, and the greenest grass in the neighborhood.)

We may as well admit, while we're really airing our dirty laundry (and there is no laundry dirtier than a broiler grower's!), that there are times when my hero and I both wonder why he didn't get into something more cheerful, like the undertaking business. He's at the mercy of hot weather, (chickens can't perspire) and windy weather (they huddle and die). He lives in terror of tourists who honk horns (scared chickens also pile up and die), and a wife who likes occasionally to serve a meal on time. He has to out-think the crafty buyer who wanders in with big deals and some other broiler house's particular brand of germ on his feet. He has to outwit even the mice bent on nesting in the feed room—all this while demonstrating the skills of an electrician, a plumber, and a chemist. He also needs the back of a stevedore and the acumen of a stockbroker.

Oh, yes, one thing more. He frequently has to make like Doctor Christian while our little chicks gleefully wade their way through every disease that poultry flesh is heir to. As a matter of record, I think he's a good medic, but I wish he'd stick to chickens. I rose voiceless one morning, and he diagnosed my case quite happily as laryngotracheitis, opining that I'd be down in my legs by night.

And oh boy, what "birds" do to our social life. Like the time we were playing bridge and held practically the entire suit of hearts between us. You can imagine what happened. A storm came up. It was "to horse and away" in the middle of a four-heart bid doubled and re-doubled. Then there was the souffle that went "soof!" because some curious cockerel stuck his head in the chain on the feed track. And can anyone please tell me if the African Queen ever made it to the sea? (We never seem to see the *ends* of movies.)

Yet all this is compensated for with (1) the selling of the birds; and (2) the CHECK. This lovely institution, however, is always preceded by a tense atmosphere similar to the Stock Exchange before Black Friday. The first sign is when my husband puts his toast in the ashtray and butters his cigarette. Then come the mumbling, the forgetting to appear for lunch, and the mailman getting waylaid for the market price sheet. Then the trucks come, the birds go, and we may as well admit it—we're lost without 'em. That is, until the next time.

Well, we're having some broiler brothers over, this evening. Six pairs of male feet will adorn my one small coffee table, and I prophesy that among conversational topics, the latest football upset will come in a poor second to coccidiosis. Then presently the six will arise as one man, go into the garage, and squat solemnly in a circle. I'll hear the car trunk open and realize, as my husband comes in for his posting kit, what I've been smelling in the back seat for two days.

Meanwhile the wives will sit in the kitchen and compare methods of holding mashed potatoes hot for three hours without drying them to the consistency of low grade shale. Then perhaps we'll play a few parlor games, such as who can raise her eyebrows highest in that "Well, what is it this time?" look.

Eventually, the husbands will come in, wash their hands at the sink, and with the most anticipatory expression possible will ask, "How about finishing up that fried chicken?"

And we will.

Don't be deceived by this carping. I'm the happiest martyr in the county from the first cheep of our day-old chicks to the adolescent crow of a three-pound chanticleer. And if the roast is ruined and the tears fall, they get dried on a tea towel that is of the finest though it may be faintly labeled BROILER MASH across the front.

Besides, we're one family that never needs to wonder what to have for Sunday dinner!

— *Marjorie Eatock*

*F*or years writers have extolled the dairy cow as a contented, generous "foster mother of mankind," or as a placid, peaceful animal.

Well, 'tain't so. All of that is pure hokum, and I wouldn't be surprised if the cow *herself* hasn't promoted the whole idea!

Actually, she's a *discontented, self-centered, greedy, excitable, cowardly slave driver*. Those are harsh words, I know. But before I'm jailed as a subversive, let me prove my point.

Heaven only knows, *the cow should be contented*. From the day she's born until she dies, she's pampered. She's taken from her mother by The Man, and is hand-fed a diet fit for a queen. She's allowed to grow into young cowhood with no responsibilities whatsoever.

And when the time comes to seek a mate, does she have to fight her way through hordes of other clinging females? *She does not.* She rolls her big brown eyes, puts on a few girlish airs, and takes a few skittish gallops. The Man rushes like mad to the telephone to arrange for love and marriage through the local artificial breeder.

A farmer who talks about the cows he owns is a dreamer. The realist knows how many cows he is owned by.

She spends a full nine months of leisure, feeling no pain, losing no breakfasts, preparing no layettes, just enjoying herself. When she has her baby, The Man and possibly The Vet, too, are there to see her through.

Meanwhile, The Man has been enjoying no such leisure. He has been footing her grocery bill with blood, sweat and tears. He has been planting feed for next year, hauling feed from the fields for this year, and doing chambermaid work for her comfort.

She doesn't just eat, she's a bottomless pit. Bales of hay, tons of grain, bushels of ensilage, gallons of water, all properly enriched, must be pitched, shoveled and carefully garnished with molasses for her.

If The Man doesn't provide for her dainty, sanitary comfort, her pal, The Milk Inspector, sees that he does.

While The Man spends endlessly on machinery to take care of these chores, the cow and The Milk Inspector (neither with a penny invested) stand by with self-satisfied smirks.

The cow is *completely* greedy. She'll go to any length to get her groceries. You'd think with *four stomachs* to keep her going, she'd be happy. Sometimes she finds too much. But unlike other animals, does she leave some for another day? Not her. She loads up all four stomachs to the point of death, just in case there might not be another chance.

She'll bawl to *get out* of the barn if she thinks there might be something edible outside. And then she invariably concludes that she's missing something and bawls to *get back in.*

She's author of the "guaranteed wage." Where else could such an idea have originated? She eats 365 days a year, whether she earns it or not, and she takes eight weeks paid vacation.

A buxom thousand-pounder, she's the world's biggest coward. A tiny heel fly can put her to flight. She'll cower at the unexpected sound of a sneeze, and a change of clothing on the part of The Man makes her *nervous.*

Any man who talks about the cows *he owns* is a dreamer; the realist knows how many cows he is *owned by.*

All family activity is planned around the cow. If The Man does get away for a breather, the cow decides how far he can go, when he must come back, and is a constant worry while he's gone.

For sheer pathos, I refer you to the sick cow. She's a master of feminine trickery when it comes to getting sympathy. She lowers her long silky lashes, rolls her liquid eyes, gets a dejected hump in her spine, and sends everyone into panic.

What does she have? *Heart trouble, cancer, the plague?* No! Just an old-fashioned bellyache, probably from trying to eat more than her share.

Generous? Hah! A cow doesn't give milk. It's taken from her forcibly, at great expense and labor.

Placid? No, again. Just plain lazy. All of the textbooks tell you how much water a cow will drink! Sure she will, *if you bring it to her*. But let bad weather come, or if the creek happens to be a long walk away. See how much she'll drink then!

She's a born tyrant, a firm believer in the caste system. Watch any herd and you'll see that there's a boss cow whose authority is *never* questioned. Any new cow in the herd is immediately challenged, and put in her place.

I've heard that a cow doesn't really sleep. This doesn't surprise me. She's much too concerned with casing the joint for places to go through fences and gates.

There probably hasn't been a lock invented even yet that'll keep a cow out of where she shouldn't be.

She's far from stupid. She can even tell time, not to accommodate you by coming into the barn, *mercy forbid*, but because she knows there's feed in there.

And never make the mistake of thinking that they're all like. On our farm we've had glamor girls, extroverts, introverts, worry warts, motherly types, business women, career girls, screwballs and nervous wrecks. But that would be another, and even longer, story.

Instead of trying to tell you *all* I know about cows at one time, I'm going to the refrigerator and get myself a good cold glass of milk.

—*Lois Rebecca Prout*

The following math won't make you any smarter, but it may help to explain why things don't always add up:

If one handy farmer can weld a broken tractor hitch in 20 minutes, how long will it take a professional welder charging $8 an hour to do the same job? *Answer:* About $16 worth.

Your brother-in-law and his wife come to visit for two weeks. He has twice as many sons as daughters, and each daughter has four brothers. You have three times as many daughters as sons, and each daughter has one brother. How many children are there in both families? *Answer:* Too many for one bathroom.

A farmer sends his wife to the implement dealer to buy two gears for the planter, a V-belt for the water pump on the tractor, four turn-buckles and six shear pins for the feed grinder. The gears cost $15 each, the V-belt costs $2 and the shear pins cost $4.20 a dozen. How much did she spend? *Answer:* $2.10 for the shear pins. The planter is obsolete and the dealer suggested locating a junker somewhere for parts. She couldn't get the V-belt because she didn't have the number of the old one, and she forgot the four whatsits.

A farmer saves $35 a week. He buys a new tractor with payments of $200 a month. How many acres can he plow before the finance company takes the tractor away? *Answer:* None. The finance company won't loan him the money to buy the plow.

A farmer catches four fish in half an hour and doubles his catch every 45 minutes. How many fish will he have in four hours? *Answer:* More than his limit and here comes the game warden.

—Bonnie Koppman

139

The Striving Years
PERSPECTIVES

The Pond

The pond was water nearly halfway to
The bottom, and the rest luxurious mud,
Cool softness we would paddle in, and do
Nothing but watch the dazzling cloudlets scud
Across the endless summer sky. To feel
The rich earth-goodness oozing through our toes
And the water's calm caress, served to reveal
To us our fellowship with all that grows.
This is a moment we remember best
There in the earth and water's kind embrace,
Stretching our thoughts to meet the sky's
   high test,
Discovering relationship to space,
Recognizing the universal bond
Between us and the earth and sky and pond.
                    Jane H. Merchant

A slow but steady rain fell all that wintry day, and froze where it fell—on the ground, the trees, the buildings. By mid-afternoon the rain had stopped, and we looked out on a glass-coated world. We were accustomed to the white, whiskery hoarfrost that often beautifies nature in winter, but this was unusual—a hard, clear coating of solid ice. Our children, ages 5 to 16, returned from school exclaiming excitedly about how good the sledding would be on the steep hill in the pasture.

Now, when our children find something so wonderful they want to share, we go with them.

They took out at once. But they never reached their destination, for between home and hill lay a gently rolling, treeless meadow. Here the children found that their sleds would speed over the ice from fence to fence with only the weight of their bodies to keep the sleds going.

What fun they had! When they came home to chores and supper, they raised an excited chorus: Dad and I must come down to the pasture tonight! "There's never been such slippery ice. You don't even need a hill!"

My first thought was, why should we fortyish parents risk life and limb going out on a dangerously slick night? But the children wouldn't give up. They begged until we simply could not refuse.

Gingerly we made our way to the meadow. We found it hard to walk, even with non-skid rubber footgear, and the sleds we pulled kept sliding into the back of our legs. It was cold! Father, ever the practical one, carried an armload of dry wood for the fire we'd build.

We will never forget the unbelievably beautiful sight that met our eyes when we reached the meadow. The moon and stars, shining brilliantly—as they can shine only on a cold, clear night—turned the meadow's expanse into a lake of glass the like of which we had never seen before. Nor have any of us beheld such a sight since.

We built our fire at the top of a slight incline. This was a perfect starting place for the sleds, although they didn't need any slope to keep them sliding. The ice reflected us and the flames of our fire as if it were clear water.

Again and again children and sleds flew over the ground. If two rode together, the sled went faster—so fast that the riders could barely turn it in time to avoid crashing into the fence. The littlest ones rode back to the starting point, pulled easily by brothers and sisters.

We parents envied those small riders; the hardest part for us was walking back! We did not take a turn at sliding as often as the children did, but stayed near the fire and absorbed the dreamlike magic of this night.

We all felt so good that as we started home we hardly noticed our cold feet and tired bodies. "Will the ice still be there tomorrow?" one of the children asked. "Probably not, if the sun shines," I said. And sure enough, by midmorning the ice was gone, leaving only an expanse of brown grass.

To this day, when I'm in the meadow, whether it is covered with luxuriant green of summer or the white of winter, I remember that night's wonder and magic. If, indeed, there was such a night! I retain a faint doubt, in spite of six other witnesses, for the experience seems like something conjured by a freewheeling imagination.

We parents learned something on that night . . . to enjoy a beautiful interlude when it is offered. And we learned to listen. Now, when our children find something so wonderful that they want to share it, we are less likely to put them off with "I'm busy—ask me some other time."

We go with them and glimpse their moment; we enjoy the new calf, the robin on the lawn, the bug, the butterfly. We share their excitement over a touchdown, a school play, a graduation. For now we know this:

Refuse to take the time, and you might miss something to hold in memory: perhaps a rare and perfect meeting of minds, or a magic that—like sledding on glass in the starlight—may happen only once in an entire lifetime.

—*Charlotte Carpenter*

While our Marine son Pat was in the Orient, a Japanese friend invited him to a party. The guests spent the evening sipping tea and silently enjoying the view—beautiful moon, bare-branched tree against an evening sky.

Pat was so impressed by this beauty and tranquility that after he came home he planned such an evening for the family. The setting was not at all the same, of course. Pat's two small brothers had dug a shallow cave in a big snowbank which had drifted in along the wooded road my husband follows to cut firewood. It was to this cave Pat invited us. From it we could see our woods loom to one side, each tree a huge flower of snow. On the other side the setting sun blazed a crimson approach across the snow-whitened slopes.

I had never before appreciated how really beautiful our farm is. We weren't Japanese-style silent, though! We recited Robert Frost's poems of winter; we sang, told stories and jokes.

Pat had built a fire—in a galvanized bucket, of all things—and had put nail kegs around for us to sit on. We stayed until the ceiling of our snow cave began to melt and trickle down on us.

Refreshed and renewed by this interlude, my husband Rex and I wondered if we hadn't been taking the unique offerings of our life for granted. We resolved to be more alert and appreciative.

On an afternoon in the spring, our Donna, age 9, insisted that we all go with her to the pasture to bring up the sheep. We found about 30 young lambs holding a track meet. They leaped, sailed through the air and cavorted in sheer exuberance. They cut droll antics as they tried to walk the steep ditch bank on tiny, sharp hooves. Soon they joined their mothers for the homeward trek.

As we trailed along, Donna began to sing softly: "The Lord is My Shepherd . . ."

I had never before appreciated how beautiful our farm is.

One evening Rex said, "Let's go down to the pond," and led the way. An orchestra of insects was having a tin-pan alley session. Fireflies sparkled and glowed, blinking on, off, on.

Rex began an old spiritual in his deepest voice, and we sang along. Presently from the cattails came a rumbling *chugalug*. Across the water boomed a *knee deep, knee deep*, and soon the pond area was alive with frog voices.

A child giggled; then we all burst out laughing. Instantly our frogs deserted us in silence, and they refused to sing another note for the rest of the evening!

Something to savor, and to store away in memory, can

be as common as a spider web trembling with dew. Or as spectacular as a tree that's ablaze with color—festooned with hundreds of Monarch butterflies pausing in migratory flight. When you've become alert to special moments, there is always the chance that the very next instant may bring you a once-in-a-lifetime thrill.

—*Lucille Campbell*

*L*ong ago, when we were growing up on the farm, my brothers and sisters and I had the usual run of childish fears. A big black stump looming in the shadows, or an eerie night sound, would set our hearts thudding and our feet making tracks.

Mother gradually taught us not to be afraid of the dark, and that the lightning that made us jump also meant rain for the crops. When the house would begin to creak in a storm, she'd tell us to grab a spoon and then we'd run for the "jar house."

The jar house, not 20 feet from the kitchen door, was a cave dug into a steep bank and faced over the front with native stone. It was our food cellar and, once we were inside, Mother would open a jar of peaches. We'd feast away; and when the storm had passed, Mother would say, "Thank the Lord for jar houses and peaches."

To get us over our night fears, she used to take us on strolls after dark. She never carried a lantern or flashlight, because an artificial light would dim nature's beauties. Often she'd say, "See? The darker the night, the brighter the stars."

Our favorite walk was through our pine woods toward the river. Mother allowed that only at night did the woods really come alive. When an owl hooted and we children would grab her skirts, she'd have us stand still and listen to the answering calls from other owls. She said the owls were telling each other someone was coming.

If it was springtime, we'd stop and listen to the whip-poorwill singing its night song from a bed of pine needles. We might jump again because we heard claws on tree bark; then Mother would tell us to look about halfway up the tree, and there we could see two tiny points of fire. She'd explain that this was a sight you could see only in the dark. The fire points were the eyes of a raccoon who'd sped to a safe height to look us over.

Mother taught us to love the dark—to face up to, or sit down on, anything scary.

If the moon was full, our mother would tell us to observe how the river—just a small, ordinary stream by day—became a silver ribbon in the light of moon and stars. Then we'd stand quietly to hear the waterfall. Mother said the falls had been there long before the country was settled. We'd pretend we were Indians standing motionless, alert.

If a scary-looking black stump reared itself like a dead thing in the dark, like as not Mother would sit down on it! Suddenly the stump became not a specter, but a handy resting place.

Our mother knew how warily we kids detoured the old graveyard. So when we came to that, she'd open the gate and we would all go in. There'd be a flutter of birds in the cedar bush, and maybe a surprised rabbit would stand up on its hind legs to look at us. Soon we were all brave—temporarily!—and we'd play hide-and-seek among the gravestones. Mother thought that wasn't being irreverent, just friendly.

If our mother were living now, and if she heard an atomic raid siren, probably she'd herd us all out to the "jar house" again. It's a certainty she would find some way to strengthen us, as she always did—even when the final darkness settled about her like a gentle spirit. The last words we ever heard her say were, "Tell the children to come see the stars."

—*Mark Hager*

A shaggy, pot-bellied little Shetland pony got all mixed up with our Christmas one year. I'd like to tell you about it.

Our four boys are in the pony business; you'll see that from our sign along the road, which reads: "Kids love ponies; ponies love kids."

Ponies, like children, have personalities. Major Midget, our chestnut stallion, 38 inches tall, 14 years old, is a gentleman in the hands of Eleanor, 7, but with our four boys he is full of tricks, devilish and unpredictable.

About a dozen Shetland foals are born on our farm each year. "First to see a colt gets to name it," we say, and the result is a lexicon of names, such as Dagwood, Scamp, Cheffy, and Twinkle.

Then Sparkle came along. A proven brood mare, she

was also the gentlest pony we ever owned. Jet black, she had that comfy look, with a broad and matronly middle, like Mom and Aunt Esther when they're not cinched up for Sunday.

In our six-pony hitch, Sparkle was literally our anchor mare. She couldn't be hurried.

The village kids adored her, and loaded her up with humanity on the outside, and with apple cores inside.

Village kids adored Sparkle. They loaded her up with humanity on the outside and apple cores inside.

Sparkle had horse sense. She would stand motionless while a child got out from under her chassis, but she likewise kicked the daylights, as well as the taillights, out of a boy who annoyed her colt.

One of the unwritten codes of our business is that no one shall become so attached to any pony, sentimentally, that it may not be sold. But already Sparkle had become an exception. She just wasn't for sale.

It was the week before Christmas that the Baxters came—a tired-looking father and a very, very red-headed little boy of seven. Billy Baxter's eyes were so blue, and his freckles so unanimous, that you hardly saw his limp.

We learned, in four words, why Mama hadn't come along: "His mother is dead."

The doctor had said that Billy needed some incentive to exercise. A pony might be just the thing—might become a playmate, too, to make his life less lonely.

Here was one order we couldn't fill. We didn't have any

pony that was that safe—none, that is, except old Sparkle, who wasn't for sale.

But between boy and beast, it was love at first sight—a silent communication between black mare, with her long whiskers and warm nose, and red-headed boy with eager, tense face.

Would we price the mare? The twins Ed and Art were noncommital. Robert and Harold objected. Eleanor rebelled. So we called a conference.

Could Sparkle, even in a small way, help heal the lame leg? The doctor had said yes.

But most important, could this decision become our greatest gift this Christmas—not something easy, but a genuine sacrifice of something loved?

We delivered old Sparkle on Christmas Eve. Bob and Harold went along, across the Des Moines River and over near Polk City. I was sorry we arrived at dusk, for a motherless farmstead is loneliest when night, and Christmas Eve, come on.

But a light was in the barn. We found a clean stall with fresh bedding and bright hay, and a red-headed boy.

It was then that I knew what I wanted for Christmas tomorrow: just ten sturdy legs and ten strong arms for my five children, and Mother Mabel to be waiting at dusk each day.

Something was happening to Robert and Harold, something as great and as timeless as Christmas itself. They were sensing their own participation in the fulfillment of another's dream. For now, Billy had four more legs to help him, and a friend to roam the pasture with when spring came around.

The freckle-faced boy stood—wordless—watching the pony, and I wondered if her barny-smell and loose dandruff weren't frankincense and myrrh to him.

We left Sparkle then, my two boys and I. We didn't have much to say as we rode home, but deep inside us, I know we shared something: a strange warm glow, warm enough to melt my eyes just a little.

Sometimes, I thought, great lessons are best taught in stables.

At the Des Moines River bridge we slowed down awhile, and looked back at the Baxter barn where one star sparkled down—bigger, more brilliant, and warmer by far than all the others. At least, that's what the two little wise men said who sat beside me in the truck.

—Clarence S. Hill

*E*nding the day with some pleasant thoughts has long been a bedtime ritual for our two daughters.

It started back when Sharon was 10 and Robin 7. I had worried because I'd noticed how often the children seemed to linger on unpleasant happenings just before they went to sleep. Even after relaxing baths and thoughtful prayers, I'd hear—as I tucked my youngsters in—resentful or worried outbursts: "I'm never going to play with Mary again—she bit me." . . . "Will that big dog that jumps on me be at the bus stop?" I didn't have to wonder why the girls talked in their sleep.

Now we try to handle problems as they come up during the day; but at bedtime we banish worries as I ask each child, "What was the *nicest* thing that happened to you today?"—inviting weighty discussion.

Was the nicest thing the letter from Grandma? Or was it the ice cream treat? Often their answers have surprised me. There was the time the children attended a matinee movie—a rare privilege. But my 7-year-old thought only a moment before beaming, "I climbed a big tree."

The time Sharon shopped with me for her school wardrobe, she told her father ecstatically, "We bought and bought and bought." But her end-of-day choice was "I'm so glad that you're going to be our Brownie leader, Mommy!" (That was *my* "nicest thing"!)

Since I've so often underestimated a child's sense of values, what about my own? I have begun playing the game myself. Surely the nicest thing today was the refund check from the utility company; but could that really compare with the thoughtfulness of my oldest, who cleaned up the kitchen on her own when I was in a rush?

One recent day held so many good things, I was sure I'd have a hard time deciding on the nicest. But it was easy! Robin had spent her entire allowance on a turtle for my nursery school class.

Then there are days when the "nicest thing" gets lost in a maze of small tragedies. The planned roller-skating falls through because the arena's closed for repairs. The substitution, a movie, doesn't work out because of car trouble. We have a bout with a nestful of hornets.

At bedtime after one such day, our tomboy finally brightened and volunteered, "I think the best thing was that I didn't have to take a bath."

Try our question on your children. The youngsters will end the day more happily, and they'll have peaceful dreams. You'll gain a more thoughtful insight. Besides, recalling the nicest thing is to enjoy it all over again.

—Minnesota Homemaker

*M*y husband came in from egg gathering as I was throwing an old spread over our new sofa. "What's that for?" he asked. So I explained, "I want to keep this sofa nice and clean."

The man looked skeptical. "I thought we bought the new sofa so we wouldn't have to cover up the old one." While I was trying for a comeback, he went on: "Reminds me of Link Dill's old car he traded in the other day. You know, when he took the seat covers off, the upholstery looked as bright as fresh paint. No profit to Link, though—he only got list price for it."

Too many people settle for a skim-milk kind of life.

I can read his mind like a book. He's in favor of keeping equipment in top condition, from screwdrivers to chicken feeders. But he also thinks the good things of life should be enjoyed—now. In fact, I've heard him say that too many people live a skim-milk existence; they save the cream for "special," only to have it turn sour.

He's right, too. I remember the bitter cold night we took Lucy and Joe Peters home with us after they'd been burned out. They hadn't rescued a thing. As we warmed ourselves with hot chocolate, Lucy said in a strained voice: "You know what I regret most? My Dresden tea set from Grandma."

The tea set had pink moss roses on it and you could see your fingers through the china. "I was so afraid something would happen to it, I kept it stored in tissue paper," Lucy told us. "I used to dream that some special occasion would come along and I'd use my nice china. Too late now— it's gone."

And I remember the auction that was held after our community's Aunt Becky died. Uncle Buford was going into a home for senior citizens, so all their belongings were up for sale. There wasn't much; but when one trunk was opened, a feminine chorus of *ohs* and *ahs* went up. The trunk was overflowing with Aunt Becky's handwork—crocheted and embroidered linens, lovely hooked rugs ... I thought of the bare rooms she and Uncle Buford had lived in, and how much brightness her beautiful things would have added. But Aunt Becky kept them put away "till we can get a better house." What a waste!

Then Fred and Ellen Baldwin, who have a dairy near us—they've worked hard all their lives and raised a family. Ellen has been arguing that they could take things easier. She told me, "We're going to Hawaii, as soon as I can convince Fred we can leave the place with the hired man for a week or two."

But one morning recently she found Fred unconscious on the floor of the milk room. Heart attack, the doctor said—from overwork, probably. So Fred was in the hospital for three weeks while his wife traveled miles to and from. The ranch got along—perhaps not as well as if the master mind had been there, but it didn't go broke. Ellen laments: "If only we had taken our trip, at least we'd have had more memories to cherish."

Our family's cherished memories include the camping trips we used to take into the high Sierras. We couldn't really afford trips, and it wasn't easy for Dad to be away from the poultry. So our excursions were inexpensive and of short duration. It came out how important they were, though—in a letter I've treasured since World War II, from our son Gary in New Guinea:

"As I sit here in this steaming, rotting jungle, things come to me out of the past. I can smell and feel the cold, crisp air of a mountain morning. I smell the bacon Mom's cooking on that old rock stove. I can hear Dad's ax ringing on the pine log he's cutting for the fire, and Sis is rattling the tin plates on the camp table. For a little while the darkness and the death smell are gone, and I know why it is that I am out here fighting."

My husband and I are glad we didn't put off those camping trips. We're glad we "used the cream" while we had it. And that decides me: I am putting away that old sofa cover so we can enjoy our sofa. It will be new only once, and that once belongs to us.

—*Ethlyn Gorsline*

When the big yellow school-bus comes down the street, stopping at the corners to gather up the children and whisk them away, I like to sit awhile and reflect:

How different things were when I was a child! We lived three miles from our school, and we kids—my sister Lou and I—walked every step of the way. When winter froze down, the walk was almost unbearably cold.

Mama and Grandma did everything in their power to protect us—made toe-warmers of soft eiderdown to wear inside our shoes; bundled us in sweaters, mufflers and mittens. Some days we'd carry small rocks, heated in the fireplace, to keep our hands warm for a little while anyway. Still our fingers would freeze and our cheeks would grow numb.

There was real danger of frostbite, or of some wintertime accident like slipping on the swinging bridge and falling in the icy creek. Our parents worried about us; but not too much, because they knew that a succession of neighbors would come out and "go a piece" with us.

Their confidence was justified. Seeing us Bell kids trudging valiantly through deep snow, someone (a mother, father, grandparent or older child) would come out to help us along until we'd be in sight of the next farmstead. By the same system we were affectionately relayed along the frigid trail homeward in late afternoon.

What a kind, brother's-keeper thing that was—"goin' a piece"! Even in summer, when folks came to visit, we'd

---

Our parents knew that neighbors would "go a ways" with us until we came in sight of the next farmstead.

---

walk a ways with them on their way home—as far as the big gate or the bridge.

Now, during my morning reflection, I find myself wishing I could again go a ways with someone. It would give me a good feeling to help someone along the road of life that passes by my door.

Occasionally something happens which makes me feel that I *have* walked a step or two with someone. . . .

For a number of years I worked as a public accountant. Strangers came to me with their listings of income and expenses. I've never forgotten the man who, after all the figuring was done, sat on. I made some courteous small-talk, waiting.

Soon it came out. "We had to operate on my youngest girl," he said. On and on he talked, telling about the difficult heart operation performed by a great surgeon in Chicago after other doctors had given up the case. How financial aid appeared magically, a gift from friends and neighbors. And how they—the child's mother and father—had gotten lost in the city while going from hotel to hospital. (He laughed, at last, to relieve the raggedness in his voice.)

After he was drained of the need to talk, he took a deep breath, gathered up his papers, smiled wryly and said: "I guess that's all."

This is it, I thought. This is how you go a ways. You listen while someone talks. You're *interested*.

I cannot provide a pattern or directions for this going-a-piece way of life; but it gets to be a sort of game, keeping an eye out for someone who needs the boon of companionship at a particular moment.

The game works two ways: While you are walking with someone, you also have a companion.

Our neighbors, Adela and Frank Ramsey, had a big family of strapping, broad-shouldered sons. I watched those fellows grow up and leave home—boys who'd ridden tractors and combines, laughed and wrestled all over the place. One went into law, one is teaching, another represents a farm bank.

The day Adela's youngest left for the Air Force my heart went out to her, for I have often brooded toward the day when our only son will be striking out for himself. How would Adela stand the loneliness? I must help.

So I went to visit. I found my friend matter-of-factly mixing a cake. "What's up?" she asked me.

"Oh, Adela!" I wailed, forsaking cheerfulness. "How will you and Frank stand being by yourselves?"

Adela just laughed. "What's all the fuss about? Our boys are doing important work. You think we brought them up to be parent-sitters?"

She carried her logic further: "It was Frank and I who wanted to farm, not the boys. Now that we've lost our help, we'll farm on a reduced scale. We've got plenty of good material left to cut a new pattern for living."

I well understood her example, for Adela and I are both accustomed to turning collars and making a new garment from the good of the old.

"When the boys and their wives and children come to visit," she went on, "what picnics we'll have!"

My friend had turned the tables. I had gone to walk a piece with her; instead, she had walked with me, showing how I could get over rough spots ahead.

Once, on a shopping trip to the city, I discovered a little girl trotting along beside me. Her dress was skimpy, her face no cleaner than it should be. If I paused to look in a window, she waited. As I reached my car and opened the door, she looked up at me shyly and said: "I've been making believe you were my mother."

Such a brief little walk with such a poignant ending. It showed me that sometimes we may be going a ways with someone without even knowing it.

—*Jean Bell Mosley*

*L*ike a lot of other women—and some men—I spend too much time fretting. I worry about paying off the mortgage, saving to put our daughter through college, remodeling our house so it's almost as good as the new homes our neighbors are building. I also worry that I may not be creating the atmosphere of love and security my family needs, and that I am not giving enough of myself to the community.

These anxieties and self-doubts are all too common among us 20th century homemakers. The world we live in

---

Happiness is a journey, not a destination.

---

is competitive and demanding. We feel we must be all things, must do everything, must have everything. A while back, the family relations specialist at our State University challenged us to take stock: "Do you really know what you want out of life? Or are you just being pushed here and there by pressures you are scarcely aware of?"

That caused me to do some soul-searching. What *do* I want for my family and myself? Success, of course; but most of all, happiness. And I recalled a maxim I had once memorized: *Happiness is a journey, not a destination.*

Funny, how something suddenly remembered will start to haunt you. I was still mulling over that adage the next morning as I dusted the living room. If happiness is a journey, I reflected, I certainly wasn't making the most of my trip. I was passing up a lot of little roadside enchantments while straining ahead toward bigger things.

Straightening magazines in the rack, I idly turned a page and read: "Atomic power may eventually create a wondrous world for women—free of work and worry." Maybe. But electricity and gas and gadgets haven't done it 100 percent. Besides, we may not be around for atomic housekeeping; why not enjoy *now?*

Today, I promised myself, I would not worry about those mortgages, college costs, community services or taxes. Instead, I would—and did—make a lemon pie. Everyone in our family loves lemon pie; but I'd been "too busy"—hadn't baked one for months. That morning I took my time, and I must say the finished product was a work of art: flaky crust, tart and translucent filling, fluffy meringue swirled into high peaks and lightly browned. . . . Just looking at my masterpiece made me feel exultant and fulfilled, even before the family applauded it by scraping pie plates bare. Suddenly it became important that I find time—regularly!—to produce small treats.

With such simple satisfactions we can put meaning into every day. Last week I visited the Cathers, a farm couple who had just celebrated their 50th wedding anniversary. I asked them to tell me about some of their happiest times, and Mrs. Cathers said: "The noon picnics we used to have. Our son and his bride lived in half our house, and at haying time she and I would feed the men in a shady corner of the yard. We served dinner with big pitchers of cold milk, and how the men ate! While they rested under the trees, we women visited or admired the roses together. That relaxed hour lightened the whole day."

Another friend tells me: "When Howard and I were first married, going to town on Friday evening was the highlight of our week. The stores were open, everybody was there and Main Street in our village was like a great big festival.

"Then our farming got bigger, help got scarcer and I suddenly realized it had been over two years since we'd enjoyed a Friday night in town. So this summer the children and I talked Dad into doing chores an hour early on

Friday evenings (with our help), and we've started again on our weekly outings."

A recently widowed friend just now stopped by for a visit. She said, "My husband and I both had jobs in town, but he used to beat me home in the evening. Because he loved to cook, he'd usually prepare supper. When it was ready, he never said a perfunctory 'Let's eat.' He would invite me: 'Come, let us enjoy our supper.'"

That rather neatly sums up what I've been trying to say. Life is a short journey at best. Recognizing pleasures as small as a good supper adds up to enjoyment along every mile of the way.

—*Lois J. Hurley*

NEW HIGHWAY

The old road has been set aside,
Too many curves have spelled its fate.
This new strip is the sterile pride
Of engineering. Arrow-straight,
Swift and efficiently it speeds
Impersonally across the land;
But still the old road, choked with
    weeds,
Rambles comfortably close at hand,
Sometimes peeking around a bend,
Keeping in touch, like an old friend.
                    Betty Isler

The Striving Years
RE-CREATION

Theme Song

Over and over, I have tried to say—
Or, this being much more suitable, to sing—
What trees have meant to me.
   The tremulous sway
Of their new tender fragile leaves in spring
On blossom-scented cool air, sanctified
By homeward winds and luminous sunset glow,
Has given me gentle glories, that abide
Within my heart henceforward; and I owe
Much I have learned of grace and fortitude
To bare trees beautiful through winter's stress,
And always their great tallness has renewed
And verified my faith in upwardness;
So all my songs say this: that every tree
That I have known lives evermore in me.

Jane H. Merchant

*S*am and I are an endless mystery to our also-married friends. The men can't understand how come Sam puts up with having his wife along when he goes fishing. The gals wonder why under the sun any woman would want to spend a vacation in a smelly old boat.

What they can't seem to get through their heads is that Sam and I like to fish together. For most women the ideal vacation might be waltzing dreamily on some expensive moonlit terrace. For me, it's getting up at 3 A.M. to see what the bass in the back cove will have.

That pearly, chilly three o'clock world, where timbered hills are wreathed in mist, the water is like grey-shot silk, and my husband sits at the tiller—cold and hunched, and wearing a four-day beard—looks better to me than the hectic world of a resort hotel.

Our idea of a good vacation is to head out from the dock—with all our problems five hours away at home, and nothing to do but just what we please.

We have tried, when the coffers were even lower than usual, to take our vacation at home; for, after all, what is a vacation besides relaxing from routine? But a large hollow *Ha* to that! Who can stay home and do absolutely nothing? Ten to one we end up painting the poultry house. Then there's the inescapable telephone—"I know you are on vacation, but..."

So from early March to late September our suitcase is on the ready for the first letup in our feed and broiler business. We keep our packing at a minimum—fish don't know the difference between denim and Dior. All that's really essential is our fishin' clothes, including hats. Sam's fishin' hat is a rain-soaked, droopy baseball number. I have one favorite that's the size and shape of a manhole cover, but it floats—which is more than you can say for me.

Oh happy the day we head for the southland, at least

far enough south of Iowa for the waitress to call my husband "sugah"; down where at sundown the bass snap at your plug with a sound like gunshot.

All this has been preceded by a month or so of old-fashioned finagling by me. As every wife knows, there's a time to mention taking a vacation, and a time to *not*. A time to *not* is when the broiler market is down, or when someone has left the bulk-bin trap open so four tons of feed augured down through to the broiler house floor.

We like to fish! We must like it, to take the punishment.

But leave out a man's rod and reel for him to stumble over, and after a while he gets the idea—and the fever. Then it's ho! for Highway Five, and don't anyone forget the tacklebox.

The trip down is never dull. It's familiar, though, for there are always broiler houses along the way. We stop at these as regularly as at gas stations. My husband is happy as a lark sitting on his heels in a strange chicken house 200 miles from home.

The way we get into action upon reaching our destination sets something of a record. We've been known to secure our motel, unload, buy licenses, rent a boat and be on the water with rods unlimbered in 15 minutes flat.

We like to fish! We must like it, to take the punishment. Our favorite warm weather pastime habitually has us marooned, drenched to the bone, cooked, mosquito-bitten.

We've spent long, fishless days waterbound, subsisting on hard-boiled eggs and candy lifesavers, because boat dock and food are three miles away, and any minute "they might start biting."

Fishing has its humiliations, that's for sure. Many's the time I've sneaked past the men on the dock (obnoxiously displaying full strings) with my own catch concealed in a Ritz cracker box (small size). At such times my husband pretends I'm a total stranger.

I'm not proud—I'll fish for anything! My man is the snob type. If what he lands isn't Moby Dick, he'll throw it back. He even tosses in some of mine.

I'll also fish with anything, from plugs to worms to peanut butter cookies. Don't laugh—I once caught a bluegill with a chunk of cookie. I'm convinced that to calculate fish reaction you have to be a fish. We own a lovely red lure with a propeller blade which, if I were a fish, I'd be mad for. What have I caught on it? A pickle bottle.

Even if the fish aren't biting, that's all right. We pull into a quiet cove, let the boat drift gently, and get on with other vital activities of a vacation:

Sleeping (my husband balanced in a pretzel shape on the bow seat, his cap pulled down over his nose). Daydreaming (me). And getting a sunburn (strictly me).

I'll peel for days after we get home. But as I peel, I'm remembering. I remember fishing and dawdling in small, twisted creeks with names like Sister and Jimmy and Plumb Foolish; where crystal clear water purled down over limestone at the feet of little fat fir trees. I remember pulling back to a lake dock on starry, moonless nights, with the water like purest black glass and nothing to guide us but tiny, winking, faraway boat lights.

I could go on and on. But if I hurry, I can get a chocolate cake baked for bribing a husband; and if the tackle box just happens to be sitting by the door where he can't miss seeing it. . .

Somewhere the fish are waiting for us two!

—*Marjorie Eatock*

*I*f something doesn't change in our marriage, I don't want to go on . . . My husband has only two things on his mind—himself and his farming. If you saw our family together, you wouldn't know the children and I were related to him. When he looks at us his face is a complete blank.

We happen to be tree farmers. My husband and I do all the work on our 350 rented acres. I am 24 and he is 29, our two girls are 4 and 2. Any money we get must go into more equipment; so our house is as bare of conveniences as our life is of recreation and human warmth. I don't mind going without things, and I do love my husband. But I can't take much more of being ignored as if I didn't exist.

—*Jane W.*

This letter describes a "status quo" marriage. Status quo means that nothing is happening. Cream has to be worked if it is to produce butter, and any human relationship has to be "worked" if it is to attain fulfillment.

When the first relationships of marriage become less impetuous, the need for a deeper bond should assert itself. If denied by one or both of the partners, this can be an intolerable loss. We counselors hear, over and over, from disillusioned older couples, "Doctor, help us turn back the calendar 25 years so we can have another chance." Jane's "status quo" letter should remind other young couples: Your chance is now. Keep something happening in your life together. Don't let your marriage slow down.

Ask the happiest couple you know the secret of their marriage success. Chances are, they won't have a pat answer—they've been too busy working out a good life together. But a Pennsylvanian who has been a husband for 35 years (and whose wife wears a lovely serenity) spells out their team philosophy:

"It's a matter of doing for each other what human be-

167

ings need most to have done. Giving each other the feeling *You're great!*—expressed not just in words but in subtler ways. Being on hand with encouragement, comfort, and reassurance—especially when the battle isn't going very well.

"Forgiveness—maybe tolerance is a more accurate term. It's a mark of grace to be able to overlook your partner's mistakes and disregard some of his (her) characteristic foibles. Tolerance implies a sense of humor. My wife has a healthy endowment of that! (She's been heard

---

How to keep your marriage from slowing down.

---

to say that if I had turned out to be the Prince Charming she dreamed of as a girl, I'd never have settled for her.)"

The farmer, like any other businessman, may unconsciously use the anxieties and demands of his work to evade closeness with his wife and children. More likely he's just plain dog-tired! A Kansas wheat grower's wife understands this: "During harvest and the inevitable machinery breakdowns, I give the man some special attention to show I care. I rub his back, keep the kids as quiet as possible, produce his favorite pie. . . .

"I'm specially on hand if he wants to talk. But when his workday runs from 6 A.M. till midnight, he's too worn out to talk. No, I don't starve for adult companionship—I read books. Besides, I'm busy, with gardening and cooking."

One big temptation of unhappy husbands and wives is to believe that an ailing marriage would right itself if the couple were better off financially. That's rarely the case.

Farm income is seldom reliable. An Iowa farm wife observes: "One of the hardest things for me, when I married my farmer, was not knowing how much money we'd have to spend in a given period."

So—she wishes she hadn't married a farmer? On the contrary: "At no other occupation can the family spend so much time together so rewardingly."

Attitude counts, as much as anything said or not said. An attitude of wanting to help, of emotional support, of never letting the other person feel inadequate, defeated, or to blame. (He may be at times, but so are all of us).

When a husband or wife retreats from "nearness" in marriage, as Jane's husband does, it may be that something in the other's attitude kills his capacity to feel close. Or maybe there is something in one's own personality that causes him (or her) to avoid closeness. Husband or wife, or both, may have been hurt in childhood so that they mistrust affection, perhaps fear they'll be rejected. Or perhaps one or both have just never learned how to express love.

The wife usually is the more aware that the marriage is in trouble. (If she only *imagines* it is in trouble, the marriage still needs some help.) It is she, probably, who must take the initiative to break down the barriers. She makes more opportunities to share feelings and experiences; she looks for ways to state her needs more clearly. She may well seek the help of a counseling service recommended by her doctor or minister, or the nearest public health unit.

Many men are inarticulate (a Maine homemaker calls her potato-growing husband the Silent Knight). Such a man may love his wife and children and may wish they would know it and stop worrying. But wives and children may have a great need to be told in words.

It is all too easy for a woman, hurt by what she interprets as a slight, to withhold her own affection and then brood about being lonely. Loneliness is a characteristic of too many modern marriages.

Rather than maintaining silence, it would be better by

far to come out of the corner either loving or fighting. As a Nebraska wife says, "A good quarrel, like a summer storm, can help clear the air."

If a couple can get through the silence to each other, they can begin to till a crop as important as any on the farm: the harmony and understanding that should go with two people living in true companionship and rearing a family.

—Dr. Aaron L. Rutledge

Remember how you loved birthdays when you were a child? The presents and the birthday cake, and the thrill of having one day a year that belonged to you alone, all helped to make a wonderful anniversary.

At middle age, have we forgotten we're still growing?

Perhaps most thrilling was the fact that you were a whole year older. You had a new inch to prove it when Poppa backed you up to the door jamb for your annual measuring.

But what happens to that pride in growth as we add 40, 50, and 60 years? Although we lap up the special attention we get from children and friends, we make as little fuss as possible over the number of years.

I wonder if our lack of pride for middle-aged birthdays isn't because we've forgotten that we're still growing? Although we can't point to a new inch on the door jamb, as each birthday passes we have a new set of memories, another layer of deepening experience to make us more sympathetic, more tolerant, more serene.

Surely we should be proud of adding another inch of spiritual growth—it's the most important of all.

On my most recent birthday I had a year's worth of memories—ordinary, but beautiful to me. Part of my inch for this year: a soft, sweet new grandchild; a blossomy spring when my flowers outdid themselves to please; the welcoming faces of my children when I visited them; and my "later years" leisure to enjoy such rich experiences.

I have had unhappiness, too. But part of my growth is the knowledge that no one should expect to live without facing grief, unpleasantness, and despair. The lessons about living that I've learned along the way soften such tough going.

Every birthday also adds to my ability not to worry about mistakes I've made. Next year, I'll try to remedy them as best I can; or if they are mistakes that can't be fixed, I've learned not to fret about them.

And every birthday I'm glad that I have embroidered another inch in the endless tapestry of recollection which not only records what happens to us, but gradually unfolds the reasons why.

So I *like* birthdays. And I hope I always will. The only birthday that I wouldn't be proud of would be one when I backed up to my spiritual door jamb and found that in the last year I hadn't added a single inch.

—*Mary G. Phillips*

I've bought us another farm," my husband announced one fall morning. "Forty acres on the Rim."

I dropped my best milk glass pitcher with a crash. "Vaughn Hunt, you *didn't* buy that old Parr place?" I quavered.

"That's the one. Honey, I know we said we'd never go in debt after we were 50. But this is one of the best irrigated parcels in southern Idaho." Vaughn wore that dreamy look he had worn years ago when we bought our first 80.

"It's an old, run-down, rocky eyesore!" I stormed. "Anyway, how could you take on another farm without talking it over with me?"

What is a woman to do when her man really has his heart set on owning more land?

He hadn't clinched the deal, it turned out. "I only said we'd buy if you would sign the papers. You will sign, won't you?"

That afternoon we drove over to look at the place. We stopped in a whirl of dust beside a mountain of clinkers left by a renter, and viewed the outbuildings—ramshackle barn, dilapidated chicken house and pigpen. Vaughn pointed out the field where he would plant Great Northern beans—as soon as we could get the land cleared and ditches changed. "We'll take out these old fences," he went on. "We'll plow up that old pasture and plant early spuds. . ." He said it all in one breath, as if he could do it all some morning while I made the hot cakes.

What is a woman to do when her man really has his heart set on something? I said I'd sign the papers. But I

172

griped! "Who is going to help with all this?" (Our son was grown and gone, the hired man already over-worked.)

"Well, I thought maybe *you'd* like to pick up some small rocks and help me clear out the brush?"

That did it. "I have plenty to do besides breaking my back on a no-good farm!" I yelled. But my husband looked so crestfallen that I melted. "Okay. Let's look at the house. Maybe we can rent it to help pay the mortgage." (I almost choked over that last word.)

The house didn't elate me. Lint lay like windrowed hay on the floors. Walls were cracked and smudged. Windows were broken and a hole gaped below the sink.

"Well, hon?" Having won me over, Vaughn was eager to get the Rim farm in shape.

We tackled the house with soapsuds, carpentry and paint. In a week we put an ad in the paper— *FOR RENT: Five-room modern house in the country*—and had 16 phone calls the first day!

Winter came, and bone-chilling winds swept down from the Sawtooth Mountains. When Vaughn and I went to carry rocks and clear away brush, we pulled our camp trailer to the Rim for shelter during lunch and coffee breaks. The short winter days seemed hardly begun when they ended and we'd take my aching muscles home to bed. But Vaughn . . . each night he'd fall into contented, snoring slumber during which he no doubt dreamed of new fields flourishing with top-price beans and potatoes.

One December day we were working over a pile of old felled trees and Vaughn said, "Hey, there's good apple-wood here. Let's cut it up for the fireplace." We have always sawed wood together, the 29 years we've been married. We have worked off many a petty difference that way. The clean sound of a sharp saw cutting through wood, and the cold bite of the wind . . . these good things will linger with us.

When you work hard at something, it grows on you.

One day, as we sat inside the trailer sipping hot coffee and eating thick sandwiches, I looked out at the view. Lava rock cliffs dropped away to the winding, willow-fringed Snake River. Snow had started to fall; the flakes made mobile, crystal-white patterns against the canyon walls. "It's beautiful," I said, and Vaughn, busy with his plans, answered absently: "Tomorrow I'm hiring a bull-dozer—to level for spring planting."

"Level!" I echoed. Friends had told me that the bulldozing on their farm had cost a small fortune!

Spring came, cold, wet and windy. Leveling the new farm had uncovered a million more rocks; so I bounced along in the trailer behind the tractor, helping Vaughn haul them to the Rim. But our tenant house was vacant again; and the afternoon we re-advertised it, I took time off to stay home and answer the phone.

I had a leisurely bath—even did my hair and nails. When my husband came in for supper I had the house rented and had put on my frilliest dress. Vaughn looked at me strangely. "We having company?" Then he put his arms around me. "Ummm, you smell good," he mumbled in my hair. "You know what? That bean field on the new place will be ready to irrigate by May."

And it was ready. We also planted 12 acres to grass and mixed grain. Then a new problem: Rock chucks came swarming up from the lava rock, hungry after months of hibernation. Soon we had the fattest rock chucks and the thinnest wheat on the Rim. "But don't worry," Vaughn said, "I'm getting a new gun tomorrow, and then we'll thin out those varmints."

The new gun—a 222 Sako rifle with a 'scope—cost about $185. This place was calling for a lot of fringe investments!

Time goes by. Our crops grew and matured. The contract beans brought a fancy price. The renters stayed on. In the fall we made a nice payment on the mortgage.

A couple of times a week now, I slip over to the Rim and enjoy our panorama. Westward, following the Snake, I see the emerald green of hayfields and orchards; to the north snow-capped mountains, touched with pink at sunrise. Upriver I hear the roar of Auger Falls, and close by I see our own Rim waterfall.

Lately I've been carrying a sketch pad and paints. I am going to have an oil painting for our next county fair. And I dream of our building a home on this spot.

Vaughn dreams, too. He has a fabulous cattle-feeding program worked out, made possible by these added acres. The figures he shows are fantastic—I can't believe we'll really make all that money! But then I didn't believe we should buy this forty in the first place, and I was wrong—dead wrong.

My husband has a new sense of security, for now he has a setup big enough to promise profit. How glad I am that we bought our "mortgage with a view." It has brought new enthusiasm to both of us. It has also proved that we two can still meet a challenge, and that together we can conquer it.

—Elsie D. Hunt

The Rewarding Years
KIN AND COMMUNITY

Need for Neighbors

Men never set such store by neighbors. They
Can live contented far from humankind
The seasons round. Some instinct they obey
Goes seeking new frontiers, leaves old behind.
But women pioneering on strange land
Have need, always, to see one chimney's smoke
Along the lone horizon. They can stand
Rough living, knowing there are neighbor folk.

Velma West Sykes

*J*ust as predictably as the cicada arrives, so does the appointed Sunday in July or August when the family clan gathers to water its roots. Everything about the annual reunion is pleasantly predictable.

If you have children beyond the age of ten, there will be an inevitable difference of opinion on the day's activity. My sons think a motorcycle race is a good reason for not going to a family reunion. Their Dad does not. (Obviously it's Dad's family that's reuning.)

Children are usually bewildered by the assemblage of people at a reunion. Once when we were encouraging a thumb-sucking 4-year-old to "go off and play with (his) cousins," he said, "Those aren't cousins; they're girls!"

Everything about a family reunion is pleasantly predictable.

They always get more of "How you've grown!" than they want to hear; and young ones are mistaken for their older brothers and sisters.

These family conclaves give aunts and grandparents great opportunity for comparing cousins and seeing atavistic resemblances: "Those are the Heinzerling eyes!" or, "They've both got Great Grampa Henry's nose."

When you're secure enough in your choice of a boy friend (or girl friend) to bring him to these family affairs, the misery diminishes. If that swain is smitten enough to endure your kinfolk, then you may judge that he's "hooked." But it's when you return with your first-born, equipped with high chair and walker and small pans for heating baby food, that you really belong.

The prime mover behind the family reunion is usually

some long-suffering female. She keeps addresses, sends out invitations and probably will be the family historian.

It is always Mother who struggles early over a hot stove to make the meal possible; it is the act of "breaking bread" together that is basic to the family reunion. The same people often bring the same things year after year. The Leimbachs always take a kettle of corn-on-the-cob and a basket of melons. The children look forward to somebody's tray of homemade candy, but the family that really wins their hearts is the one with a trunk loaded with soft drinks cooled in a big washtub.

The family reunion is the annual forum for news, and so "visiting" is its principal preoccupation. Where is George living now? . . . How many children does Dan have? . . . How old is Mary? . . . Is Judy going on to school? We evaluate one another's achievements; we find out what we've done. Conversation glides smoothly over the events of life lived, but unfortunately, seldom dips beneath the surface to share what it means.

We seldom use our common ancestry to help reveal our common humanity. Instead of asking, "What have you done since we saw you last," we probably should be asking, "What has life done for you?"

What the aunts consider to be indiscretions—divorces, illegitimate pregnancies, drinking problems, family fights, etc.—will be scrupulously avoided, unless, of course, all parties remotely concerned are absent. You won't hear anyone claiming the guilt in phrases like, "It's the old Leimbach lust coming out," and *that's* for sure! We all wall off our weaknesses like malign cancers.

In late afternoon when surface conversation has been exhausted, the ball game is deteriorating and the children have finally discovered they have more in common than last names, the party breaks up.

There is a gathering up of picnic baskets and folding chairs and ball gloves, and a saying of farewells with promises never kept to "get together more often."

During the drive home we rehash the whole day, pooling the news from separate conversations, straightening out puzzling relationships. Our teen-ager wants to know how closely we're related to those "cool" girls from New London. Another is full of questions about Uncle Nelson's wooden leg. The third one brags about how much pop he drank, and then comments with pleasure, "Gosh, I never knew I was related to Marty" (a friend made previously through other channels). "How's come we don't ever go to see them?"

How's come we don't? There's no one good reason. Life just doesn't allow us to "keep" all the people we'd like to keep. And that's probably why we persist with family reunions, trying to hold onto the thread of relationships once very important, trying to pass on to our children that sense of having derived from somewhere—of having a responsibility to a tradition, and hoping this responsibility will give life a little more meaning.

—*Patricia Penton Leimbach*

*D*own in the pasture at Grandpa's was a straw stack, a mountainous one that drew us kids like flies. Other grownups would say we were ruining the stack, but Grandpa would just laugh, a big booming laugh, and say: "Keeping a youngster off a straw stack is almost a sin. Why, it's like keeping water away from a thirsty man."

There was Grandpa for you. He was a big, bald-headed man of Irish-Swedish-German descent, with a white cowhorn mustache. His hands were as big as hams, and his voice boomed like a 12-gauge shotgun. The whole house seemed to shake when he laughed, and the more grand-kids he had around him, the louder he laughed.

I recall how we used to drive up the hill to Grandpa's big house in our Model T sedan. The yard overflowed with relatives' cars; dogs and cousins ran in every direction.

Grandma was there, small, quick, loving a houseful of kinfolk to pamper and fuss over. (She had eleven children.)

Grandma loved a houseful
of kinfolk to fuss over.
But it was Grandpa
who made it a magic place.

But it was Grandpa who made it a magic place.

I remember one Sunday when about twenty of us cous-ins chose up sides and went down into Grandpa's cotton patch, and started a cotton boll fight. The bolls were at that hard stage before they opened, ideal for chunking, as hard as green apples and almost as big. Best of all, they'd sting when you were hit, but wouldn't break the skin.

We were having a regular war, when two of my uncles ran up and ordered us out.

It seems like yesterday. Grandpa yelled from the barn. It was half a mile away, but you could have heard him twice that far, and he hollered: "Leave those kids alone." Afterwards, I heard him say: "They could throw for an hour and not destroy over four or five dollars' worth—and they're having a thousand dollars' worth of fun."

My mother and aunts used to complain that Grandpa spoiled us. I once heard him tell my mother: "A little bit of fussing won't hurt him near as bad as not giving him love and affection. It's the neglected ones who usually turn out bad. When a youngster grows up and gets out on his own, he can outgrow an awful lot of petting and spoiling in a hurry."

I remember one Sunday afternoon at Grandpa's when the crowd wasn't as gay as usual. One of my cousins, a pretty girl of eighteen named Leona, had eloped with a young share-cropper the night before. My aunt felt that her daughter, for whom she had many plans, had married beneath her. Grandpa was quiet while my aunt talked and cried. Finally, she asked Grandpa if she should try to have the marriage annulled.

Grandpa said: "Well, honey, if you ask my opinion, I'll give it. It appears to me that your only objection to this young fellow is that he doesn't have lots of money. A man can acquire money much easier than he can acquire a kind heart, a good personality, or the will to work. I know this young fellow, and I figure Leona did a good day's work when she hooked him. He will be good to her, and he has enough backbone to make a decent living. My advice to you is to stop sniffling around."

Grandpa was the sort of fellow who never talked about his neighbors. If he couldn't say something good about anyone, he'd never mention their names.

Often when Grandpa's big living room was filled with relatives, someone would repeat some gossip. That was when Grandpa would cut in on the conversation. Loudly and almost rudely he would change the subject. The ones who had been gossiping would instantly realize that they had broken the unwritten rule of Grandpa's home, and would drop the subject.

Those Sunday dinners at Grandpa's were something I shall never forget. His smokehouse was always filled with cured hams and bacon. His cellar held stores of canned and dried fruit and vegetables.

The massive dining table would comfortably seat twenty people. Every Sunday from two to five tables were served before our large clan had all eaten.

Grandpa sat at the head of the table like a commanding general. He left his chair only long enough to call the next tableful to their positions. He said grace at each table.

It was often 2 P.M. before we kids were called, hungry as coyotes, to the last table. Grandpa would step out on the porch and yell, "You young'ns, come on and wash up." We'd come running and yelling like a band of Apaches.

After we'd wash, we'd all file past Grandpa and hold out our hands. If they weren't clean enough, he'd send us back to the porch to wash again.

Grandpa would wait until the last table to eat with us. He'd sit and visit with the grownups while they ate, but he never took a bite until the last of his clan had been seated. While we stuffed ourselves on cake and whipped cream, he'd sup big cups of hot, black coffee, and smoke his pipe. He kept us laughing during the whole meal. He had a way of making every kid at the table feel that he was an important member of the family. He had a special joke and a special nickname for each child.

Grandpa tried never to show favoritism among his grandchildren, but I always suspected that I was his favorite. Now, I realize that someone with a heart as big as Grandpa's could make everyone feel that he was special.

Grandpa left us in 1935. Many people were surprised that his estate was so small. However, drought and depression had forced him to put a heavy debt on his land. More important, I think, he had used his money to help members of his family out when they were hard up.

But Grandpa left me a fortune. I think he has helped me to be a better Dad, and some day to be a better Grandpa. He has made me see the riches there are in laughter.

—*Josh Drake, Jr.*

*T*here's something heart-wrenching about seeing your son stand at the altar with a vision of femininity in lace and net, no matter how much you have learned to like the girl of his choice. It strikes home like a poisoned dart that he doesn't need you anymore! The preacher reads lines from the wedding service: *Therefore shall a man leave his father and mother. . .*

You think of that empty maple bed in the boys' room upstairs, and the closet that's suddenly bare of sloppily hung and heaped-up clothing. You try not to remember

---

I said I was going to treat our son's new wife as if she were my own daughter.

---

how he always slept, with the blankets over his head and huge bare feet sticking out at the bottom.

Determinedly I pushed away these painful thoughts and concentrated on the bride. Poor girl, now *she* would be the one down on all fours to fish for his socks—rolled in tight balls and far back under the bed.

I'd been forewarned of this moment of relinquishment during our son's junior year at college, when the picture of a new face appeared on his bureau at home one weekend. Intuition told me that this was *the* girl. Little by little Son told Dad and me about her. She liked music and books, went to his college. She liked all sports except baseball, his favorite, about which she didn't even know a bunt from a home run, he glumly confided. . .

Our new daughter-in-law had been too busy growing up and going to school and working part-time to learn much about cooking. But she had what was necessary: intelligence and a good basic cookbook. Although I had baked 18 loaves of bread a week for the last 20 years, plus enough pies, cakes and cookies to reach around the equator, I vowed to myself that I wouldn't offer advice unless she asked for it. (Sometimes she does consult me—to make me feel valuable, I suspect.)

I also refrained from telling her the way Son likes tomatoes fixed, or that he considers baked potatoes an insult and can make an entire meal on nothing but buttered squash. Her father-in-law is living proof that weak coffee, dough balls in the gravy and pie crust like whang leather aren't fatal to a new husband, although the same fare years later might cause a domestic split that would make the Grand Canyon look like a creek.

But, try as one will, it is nearly impossible for a mother-in-law not to sound like a mother-in-law on occasion. I slipped up at least a couple of times. When Son and his bride each left his own church and both joined a third, I cried, "How foolish! Your faiths are so much alike, why did you both give up?" I can see now that joining a third quite similar denomination was an ideal compromise. Another time I dropped in on my daughter-in-law while she was shining her husband's shoes. "My son was brought up to shine his own shoes. I've never polished his dad's boots," I steamed.

"Please, Mom," she said quietly. "Between classes, study and job, he puts in a 16-hour day. I'd rather shine his shoes and have him sleep 10 minutes longer."

She was right, and I had the grace to say so.

But my first slip-up was when I said I was going to treat Son's new wife as if she were my own daughter. He set me right: "You can't, Mom, because she *isn't* your own. We're a whole new world to her."

No two families are alike. For example, although friendly teasing and harmless practical jokes have been a way of life for us, we soft-pedal that kind of nonsense

185

with the new member. Our own daughter delights in running hot water at the kitchen sink so her brother's shower will run cold; but she'd never pull that trick on her sister-in-law. Also, since Son's wife is city-bred, we respect her right to be skittish about anything that crawls, wiggles or squirms, especially newborn kittens.

I won't pretend I didn't worry when Daughter-in-law spooned cereal down our grandson at age six days. But by the next morning, after Baby had slept the night through, I was sorry I hadn't had some of the same stuff for my babies, including Grandson's daddy.

Our young grandson will need reprimanding now and then, and I've been happy to observe that his mother has a fine, healthy though controlled temper—something no mother can operate competently without. I suspect that she won't be above switching his legs when he needs it. (When that happens, I'll probably cringe and then nonchalantly whistle "Dixie," as my mother used to do while her grandkids were being punished.)

It is a blessing when two women who love the same man—one as his mother and one as his wife—are compatible. For surely there is no person more miserable than a man who finds himself caught in the cross-fire between a jealous mother and a resentful wife. It's a struggle in which no one can be the winner.

More and more I understand how young people resent the ties that bind, even—especially—in the name of maternal devotion. On the other hand, I'm glad that my smart young daughter-in-law hands over her husband now and then for a bit of mothering.

Just a bit, mind you. The way she's spoiled that guy, I wouldn't want him back for long!

—*Ethelyn Pearson*

*I*n December, most of the families we know draw together toward the light and warmth and shining perfection that is Christmas. It is almost as if hearts joined hands to round out the circle of family and friends, welding the weak spots that a year's neglect or buffeting brings.

Our circle closes, centering around the symbols of love and affection: the Christmas Story, a gilded tree, presents, the big dinner, church music. For a little while, faces—and hearts—turn inward to the warmth and comfort of belonging.

Behind our backs, the light escaping through our snug circle reveals the faces of the world—the human family . . . the millions striving in a frail way to join hands in

---

It is good to warm one's heart in the family circle.

---

an imperfect sphere. But each pair of outreaching hands belongs to a man or a woman or a child. Within each person, whether he roams the steppes of Mongolia or is jostled by the throngs in New York . . . within each being exists the same mystery of the human soul and mind.

There is a oneness in the human family. The kind of oneness that makes any woman wakeful at night if her child is ailing . . . that makes her grieve when he grows up and leaves her household . . . makes her proud if he achieves. The same feelings, no matter whether a woman lives under a thatched roof or in a Kansas farmhouse.

And there is at the same time a loneliness in every being. No matter how great the love, how clinging the handclasp, how warm and close the circle . . . each human being has the fathomless comprehension that he is, in the final analysis, alone.

Look at the faces of the world, remembering: All know gaiety and sorrow as well as you and yours; all have experienced birth, hunger, love, and the prospect of death; all need beauty, worship, work in some degree . . . while each is a lonely captive within his own self.

It is good, in this season, to warm one's heart in the familiar circle of family and friends. But this is also a season to turn our circle inside out and share its warmth with the human family in the shadows.

When each small, snug circle faces out allowing its light and strength to flow outward, then the heart of the world will be warm.

—*Gertrude Dieken*

It's hard to say just when we started leaving the upstairs hall light on all night. It must have been when one of the children was ill. Whatever the reason, it has been burning now for about seven years; it can burn another seven, and I'll be glad. It wasn't really late last night when a soft knock at the door had my husband Dwight out of bed and into his slippers. The apologetic knocker was a young man out of gas. "I saw your light," he said, "and thought someone was still up." He didn't have to explain. There had been so many others.

There was the blizzard back in 1954. Dwight had spent all afternoon rescuing school busses with the tractor.

When we banked the furnace for the night, I was thankful that the awful day was behind.

I didn't want to wake up, to admit there was someone at the door, but when I heard Dwight's feet hit the floor, I knew what would happen: He'd throw some wood in the furnace, maybe brew some coffee, ask the stranger to warm himself while he put on heavy clothes and got the tractor and chains.

I could smell the wood smoke and hear the coffee gurgle. In the fuzziness at the edge of sleep, I seemed to see

---

Helping out was something any decent person would do.

---

the way Dwight's father used to cozy the grey granite coffee pot with gentle, weathered hands after getting up at night to help round up the neighbor's sheep. Grandpa had carved the mold from which my husband was formed. So much alike those two! Neither would ever admit to owning a tender heart; helping out was something any decent person would do.

As Dwight crawled back into bed, he said, "The poor guy was nearly frozen. He got turned down one place because their tractor wouldn't start. Then he saw our light. . . ."

Our farm is at the edge of a community of a dozen families. The house was built as a "mansion house" by the original homesteader, and though our idea of a mansion differs a bit from his, we're glad he built next to the road, instead of at the center of the section. I'll admit, though, that at 2 A.M. I'm not so sure.

One foggy night last fall, three husky young men in mackinaws came banging at our door. Still half asleep, I thought of escapees from the penal institutions which flank our county. But it turned out to be college boys getting initiated into a fraternity. They'd been blindfolded and driven for miles, then let out with orders to take off the blindfolds and walk back. They saw our light.

"Why didn't you offer to drive them to Mt. Gilead so they could catch a bus?" I asked.

"Because they were supposed to walk!" said Dwight, surprised that I'd considered anything else.

If it's raining when the nocturnal knocking begins, we just assume that someone's cows are out. (The moon may drive human beings to lunacy, but it's rain that drives cows to madness.)

It happens over and over, like a recurring dream. As I feel for my shoes, the voice at the door asks: "Do you have Holsteins? About 25 of them just went across the road. I saw your light and thought if they weren't yours, you'd know whose they were."

The absolute darkness of such a night defies description. Except for the occasional flash of lightning, it would be useless to try to find the cows. They move like grotesque ghosts. I stumble.

On the way home, I announce firmly, "That light has got to go!"

"What light?" Dwight asks.

"The upstairs light. Everybody sees it and stops."

"Don't be silly. They were our cows this time."

There are three distinct knocking categories. The first is knock, wait, and knock again, which we have learned means: "I'm sorry to bother you, but I need help." The second is a persistent pounding: "Something is wrong. I'm doing you a favor by stopping to tell you. Hurry and get up so I can be on my way." The third is a frantic banging accompanied by calls for help. When this kind comes, don't plan on going back to bed!

Suzanne, our oldest girl, was the first to hear Evelyn

Langoehr knock. I heard Evelyn call, "Suzanne! Get your Mom and Dad up! Our house is on fire!" From the window I could see flames coming from under a corner of their roof. Dwight grabbed buckets, and I managed to get the telephone operator and yell "Fire at Langoehr's!" Then we dashed for the burning house. The neighbors formed a bucket brigade up a ladder and across the kitchen roof. One of the men became confused and instead of handing the bucket of water to Karl Langoehr, he threw it at him.

The volunteer firemen were able to limit the fire to the upstairs, but by the time the fire was under control, the sun was rising. I went home to fix bacon and eggs and coffee for the Langoehrs, while other neighbors made sleeping arrangements for the displaced family. We were thankful we'd left our light on *that* night.

The light has let us share some unforgettable moments with others. When Ida Garverick got word that she could bring her husband Glen home from the hospital, she asked me to help them out.

I've never seen anyone so full of life, or the love of life, as Glen that day. He saw the sprouting corn, the greening wheat, the red-winged blackbirds. He waved to farmers in the field, reached over and touched the horn when we passed a friend along the road. I drove more slowly than usual because he seemed to enjoy the ride so much. "Has Dwight started on his bean ground? I'll bet my garden is full of weeds! Have you used any lettuce yet?" He hardly waited for an answer.

At home he stationed himself on the porch swing, stopping every passerby, hungry to be a part of the surging life of spring. I believe that must have been the happiest day of his life.

It was only eleven thirty that night when the pounding came—frantic, incessant pounding that sent us racing for the door.

It was Ida. We knew then the worst had happened. A

sudden relapse and Glen had died.

"We'll be right over," Dwight's voice was firm and reassuring. The rest of the night was a haze of long-distance calls and of decisions to be made. But for us, it was a night of relearning that it's a privilege to be near someone we love like Ida when she needs us. Our other neighbors, too, came in, to say by their presence the things that words too often fail to convey.

It was still dark when Dwight and I walked home, hand in hand, guided by the dim glow of the hall light.

There were other times, many more: when a car skidded on loose gravel, overturned and pinned a boy beneath it; when the bread truck dangled over the bridge abutment; when a fire started in Beck's pine trees. And there were times when we needed help ourselves, and found it—in the same people who'd come to us when they'd been in need of friends.

Gradually over the years we have come to realize that our upstairs light has lit a bigger light in our own lives— one we never want to turn off. It means too much to us.

—*Dorothy Predmore*

AS OTHERS SEE US

*Why is it that each time
    I err
In ways that seem to me
    quite new
My friends and relatives
    all say,
"How typical of you"?*
        Marcia Hamilton

*O*ur burro Joey is—let's face it—a dyed-in-the-hide rascal. So no wonder I worried that Christmas when he . . . but to tell you about that, I must fill in the background.

Grandpa (my father) bought Joey—ordered him from a catalog outfit—when the donkey wasn't much bigger than a jackrabbit. Grandpa had retired from country preaching; now that he and Grandma didn't have a congregation to look after, they went in for pets. And how Gramp loved that little animal!

But after a couple of years' growth Joey got to be too much for Gramp to handle. So my husband Ralph and I went over and loaded the beast in a trailer and brought him here to the farm.

Many's the time I've regretted that impulsive act. But the children were delighted. Now they had something to ride. They thought!

But Joey had no plan to become a beast of burden. He used every trick in the book. He'd make for the nearest tree and rub Ernest or Mark or Dorothy off his back—or maybe it would be teen-age Cora Beth. Or he'd take off pell-mell, then come to a quick stop and put his head down so his rider would go scoot-sliding into the dust.

And bite! Till the kids learned to muzzle Joey with a strap around his nose, young arms and legs stayed raw from being nipped. Only Barbara, our college-age oldest, survived unscathed; she was too dignified to bother with the scamp.

But then, imagine Barb's feelings when Joey riddled her favorite school dress—practically ate it off the clothesline. He was out in the grove that day, with a fence between him and the clothes. There was a high wind; the dress, flapping merrily toward Joey, offered a game of tag. And so did a couple of my best percale sheets!

The list of Joey's misdeeds would fill a book. He was always breaking fences and finding new mischief. He nosed the lid off the cream cooler and upset the cans. He invaded the hen house. (Have you ever heard a donkey sing? Add that to the commotion a hundred terrified hens can make, and you have pandemonium.)

By now you are wondering why I didn't call the rendering truck to take Joey off our hands. Many's the time I threatened to! But our youngsters were crazy about him; they never gave up the notion that "any day now" Joey would start behaving like a gentleman.

And they held Grandpa over my head: "Mom, it'd break his heart if anything happened to Joey." They spoke the truth, too. Gramp was, in fact, so attached to Joey that

---

Gramp was so attached to Joey that we'd kept the burro's sins a secret from him.

---

we'd more or less kept the burro's sins a secret from him.

Well, a few weeks before Christmas, matters came to a head. Suddenly there was our Cora Beth in a walking cast (bone separation, from Joey's crushing her ankle against a tree). And she was scheduled to be Mary the Mother in the Senior Class Christmas Tableau.

The ankle-crushing episode kept me tied in knots one whole sleepless night, and next morning I put my foot down: "That animal has got to go!" Never had I meant anything more. The family, including my good-humored husband, lapsed into gloom; but I stood firm, ignoring moans and tears as I shooed the children off to school.

I meant to call that rendering truck! But Grandpa was coming to supper (Grandma being away on a visit), and I thought, well, I'd tell him a truth or two and *then* I'd get

194

rid of Joey. . . .

That afternoon our Gramp was perched on the kitchen stool settling the affairs of the world while I peeled the potatoes. He looked peaked, I noticed; but that wouldn't keep me from telling him about Joey. I was just about to—when the door burst open and our younger schoolagers exploded into the room, with Cora Beth hobbling at the rear in her cast.

"Mom! Gramp! Guess what!" Mark shouted. "Joey's going to be in the Christmas play!"

You could have floored me with a breath. "Joey's going to *what?*"

"He's going to be the donkey that Mary rode to Bethlehem before the Baby Jesus got born in a stable," Dorothy explained.

Before I could open my mouth to yell *No, a thousand times no,* Grandpa, beaming all over his face, got in the first word: "Always knew that Joey had talent. Let's all take some carrots out and congratulate the little fellow."

But I detained Cora Beth in the kitchen. "Now let's get the straight of this," I said.

Cora Beth said, well, Mrs. Lorenz (the teacher who arranges the tableau every year) had an *inspiration.* Wouldn't it be dramatic to have a real live donkey in the play—for Mary to ride, like in the Bible story? And somebody piped up, "Cora Beth's got a donkey!" And so that was settled.

"How're they going to get Joey up the school steps?" I argued. "Also, who's to keep him from wrecking the scenery and fracturing your other ankle?"

Cora Beth didn't have the answers, but everyone else seemed to. Frank Pratt, the boy who was to be Joseph and lead the donkey, would come over and ride Joey around to soften him up for his role. My husband said *he'd* build high sides on the 4-wheel trailer and haul Joey to the schoolhouse. Stairs? No problem! Furthermore, we'd keep

Joey from his feed for 24 hours, so he'd mind his manners and munch alfalfa during the tableau.

So I gave in. I couldn't be the one to dim Grandpa's pride. Maybe something whispered the truth that this would be the very last Christmas we'd have him with us.

And that's how it happened that, the evening of our Redwood Falls High School's annual Christmas program, I sat with husband Ralph, Grandpa and Grandma in the carol-filled auditorium—my ears straining for backstage uproar. I almost wished Joey would hurry and do his worst, and end the suspense.

Grandpa kept whispering, "When does Joey come on?" and I kept explaining that the seniors' Nativity scenes were *last* on the program.

Inevitably the moment arrived. Gray curtains closed onstage for a backdrop, silence fell, darkness swallowed the auditorium. The spotlight searched out robed, slowly moving figures, a shaggy gray head with great long ears.

You've never seen anything to surpass the humble dignity of that journey across the stage. As Joseph (Frank Pratt) led our little burro, step by step, Joey seemed to sense that, like the donkey of old, he carried a precious burden. And so he did—although Mary the Mother was really our Cora Beth, sitting her steed a bit nervously.

A great sigh—mine—went up from the transfixed audience as Mary and Joseph, plus Joey, vanished into the wings. A few moments later, while the choir joyously heralded the birth of a King, the curtains parted on the tableau. Mary, her face aglow over the manger . . . Joseph looking down worshipfully . . . and there was Joey, contentedly munching hay in his "stall"—unconcerned as shepherds and Wise Men added their adoration.

So our ornery little burro had turned over a new leaf? Well, I have to be truthful. The curtains had barely closed when Joey gave out with a loud *hee-haw*!

The way I figure, that proves how human our burro is.

Most of us revert to type after a spell of nobility. But you should also see how Joey (humanlike) reverted to the *good* again these last three Decembers . . . to play his big role in our Christmas program.

—*Georgia Parker*

I shall always remember one Saturday in mid-winter when the snow was drifted as high as the eaves of the barn. We had to drive to Spiritwood in Dakota Territory for groceries, and since father worked in Jamestown, my oldest sister Helen, 16, was teamster of the family. She hitched up our horses to the sleigh while Mother bundled us all to the eyes in warm clothes and settled us on the hay in the box, with hot bricks under the heavy robes around us.

Town, eight miles away, was a real treat. We shopped, picked up our precious mail, and then set out for home in

---

Before the night was over
seventeen other lost, frightened
people came to the door.

---

the sleigh, sucking striped peppermint sticks that the grocer had given us. The sun shone, the snow sparkled, the sleigh bells jingled.

Suddenly the sun was blotted out by heavy wet snow. It was a prairie blizzard: no visibility, no sense of direction,

197

the wind whirled, seemed to blow from all directions at once. The horses stopped, refused to go on. Their eyes were frozen shut, they had lost the road and were up to their bellies in drifts and on the point of panic.

Helen talked to them, thawed their lids and quieted them, then led them back on the road. They went well for awhile but eventually they were plunging and snorting again and in snow so deep they could hardly move.

By now it was early dark, the robes were heavy with snow, the children were crying. People had been lost before, Helen knew, and not found until the spring thaw. She stood petting the horses.

Then, away in the distance, like a star shining feebly, she thought she saw a light. She knew what she must do. Guiding the horses back onto the road, she led them, talking to them as she floundered ahead, finally reaching a one-room house. Hearing sleigh bells, the man of the house rushed out, carried us small children into the warm little house and put the horses into the barn. We had come upon the honeymoon home of a young couple we knew well. The little bride fixed a good lunch; we were warm and happy.

Before the night was over, seventeen other lost, frightened people came to the door, guided by the light in the window. The children slept crosswise on the honeymoon couple's only bed; the grownups played cards and sang as the storm raged outside.

When morning broke, the storm was still roaring and no one dared venture out. The wind moaned like a lost soul. Yet inside was the spirit of a party; people shared the store-bought groceries, cooked favorite recipes and visited. For years they talked of "Mattie and George's party" as something wonderful.

The storm lasted all day; sometime in the night it blew itself out. The morning was bright and bitterly cold. After a good hot breakfast, families prepared to start back home. The men shoveled drifts from doors and windows, and we caught sight of a beautiful new world, deep in sparkling snow. After fervent "good-byes" the first sleigh started out. When our turn came, the road was broken and we reached our own dooryard easily.

It was only then that we children remembered our beloved canary, left alone at home. We knew he must be dead, for the fire must long since have burned out. What joy when we opened the door to be met by a burst of song. The tiny bird had somehow survived the bitter cold.

Our experience was only one of many that befell prairie people. Everywhere there was a light in the windows; it could mean the difference between life and death. Pioneers with grateful hearts thanked their God who inspired those lights that reached out all night across the lonely, wind-swept prairies.

—*Sybella Pearson Wright*

DESCRIPTION OF A FRIEND

Oh, the comfort—the inexpressible
  comfort
Of feeling safe with a person;
Having neither to weigh thoughts,
Nor measure words, but pouring them
All right out just as they are
Chaff and grain together—
Certain that a faithful hand will
Take and sift them,
Keeping what is worth keeping
And with the breath of kindness
Blow the rest away.

    Author unknown

The Rewarding Years
APPRECIATION

Rain in the Wood

I like to think how glad a forest is
For rain it had been needing! Surely each
Furred creature loves the smell of it at his
Small doorway, sniffing it, just out of reach
Of its cool touch, and every inhabitant
Of a woodland must delight to hear the sound
Of rain on tree and underbrush and plant,
With all the myriad tricklings to the ground.
And sometimes, walking in a rainy wood,
I seem to hear the thirsty leaves above
My pathway whispering their gratitude—
While here and there a bird sings out its love
Of rain—and, as before a banquet spread,
The very forest seems to bow its head.

Elaine V. Emans

The Boss (that's my husband) just finished the newspaper article he was reading and let his eyes stray across to FARM AND BUSINESS OPPORTUNITIES. "Hear this," he said. 'Ranch for sale'—the owner is retiring, it says."

This hits me hard—we'll soon be retiring ourselves. Wonder how we'd word a For Sale ad.

A PRIZE—*10-acre poultry ranch on desert.*
Laying houses for 7,000 birds; 5-room adobe house,
bath, fireplace. Plenty of shade.

That's what we could put in an ad. The really important things lack cash value. Like memories. . .

About those laying hens, for instance. It was back in 1926 when, young and inexperienced, we first dreamed of poultry farming. The banks didn't have the same faith in us that we had. So my husband worked on a neighboring ranch to feed us, while I stayed home and raised children and chickens. Before work, after work and weekends, he made endless rows of 'dobe bricks from our clay-and-sand soil, and baked them in the sun—for our hens' home, not ours!

When the first laying house was finished except for installing roosts and nests, we sent out the word: "Chicken housewarming Saturday night." And people came—in jalopies, in pickups; from little ranches in the foothills and big spreads out in the valley. With youngsters!

I'll never forget those donated cakes—high and light, rich and dark—to go with the huge freezer of ice cream we had cranked up. We sat on bales of sweet-scented hay. The spacious cement floor was liberally slicked with corn meal. So we danced, two-steps and waltzes mostly, to the strains of our new phonograph that would play two 3-minute records with one winding.

The noise never bothered the children. They slept on the

hay bales, but woke up instinctively when the cakes were cut and the ice cream dished!

Our 5-room adobe house did not exactly spring up. It grew, gradually and backbreakingly, from the multitude of bricks my man made from dirt he'd excavated to make a cellar. A prospective buyer might take a dim view of the structure. Its rough-textured walls aren't precisely four-square. We regretted this recently when we tried to put washable wallpaper in the bathroom. Walls and paper wouldn't line up, so the job's a bit less than professional.

That bathroom! Our tub had faucets marked "H" and "C." But only the "C" worked—the "H" came in buckets and tea-kettle from the kitchen stove. Now, of course, our faucets

What will you bid for our farm —lock, stock and memories?

deliver what they claim to. We also have an electric heater in the bathroom. But in those days the place was never warm. The children's bodies steamed like little puddings as I lifted them out of the tub; so I'd wrap them in towels and hustle them out to the fireplace. . . .

At this moment in my reverie, my mate rises to poke a Joshua tree log farther into the fire. I suppose a stranger would notice that our fireplace smokes a little when the wind is from the east. But my husband and I remember the fun we had building it—from dark red, mica-flecked rocks we'd picked up in the Tehachapi foothills. Our 4-H Clubbers and Boy Scouts burned marshmallows over its coals, eventually brought their dates for fireside snacks.

"Plenty of shade." . . . But our ad would not describe this

place the way we saw it first! Bare, under a blistering sun, with only sagebrush to dot the dry, brown grass. Here was a home for lizards, horned toads, jackrabbits and rattlesnakes. We planted a few spindly "whips"; shielded them from voracious rabbits, carried panfuls of dishwater to moisten their thirsty roots.

Later came hard-won well and windmill; but who'd have thought that those skinny plantings of ours would ever become havens for birds—and children? Our youngsters' tree house still provides a hideaway for *their* offspring.

The buyers of our place might regard the tree house as an eyesore. "I bet they'd even tear it down," I mutter.

"Who are 'they,' and what are you talking about?" asks my husband, coming back from the cookie jar with his bedtime snack. "You've been staring into space for half an hour—don't believe you've heard a word I said."

I return reluctantly to the here and now. "Well, what *did* you say?" And the Boss chuckles: "I said I'd not swap our place here on the desert for all the dad-blasted money on earth. Our roots go too deep—we'd never transplant. One of these days we'll let younger hands take over the work, but we'll never leave our home."

I beam, and ruffle the place where his nice wavy hair used to be. Once again, as it's happened so often in our nearly half-a-century together, our minds have met and agreed before we ever got around to discussion. NO SALE!

Ethlyn Gorsline

I grew up with the idea that all women are neurotic. But one Sunday there strode into my adult Sunday School class a country school teacher whose slip was showing, but who contradicted my idea on neurosis so abruptly that, then and there, I was a goner.

She was a farm girl who, at 17, had lost her mother and had assumed much of the care of a family of seven children. She later finished two years of college, by intermittent teaching and hard work.

So, as a somewhat rusty blade of 33, I married Mabel, a tender young thing of 27. We both agree we're glad we waited until each other came along.

I never saw anyone who hated sin so much, who could still be so darned nice to so many sinners.

And I still love her. First, for her loyalties. She's loyal to me always. Although she has good cause, she never mentions my glaring weaknesses before the children, something too many mothers do; they jealously covet first place in their youngsters' hearts.

She is loyal to my business and can discuss it intelligently. She is sensitive to the success or failure of the crops. She isn't above having a box of new-born pigs or an orphan lamb on the dining room register.

In my absence, she directs work without a hitch, because she cooperates with the hired help and their families, and treats them as the equals they are.

No high-pressure salesman ever sells her a "bill of goods." She's a partner in actuality as well as in name, shares the business and the bank account. This settles that old "allowance problem."

She likes my hobbies—my trees, guns, pony herd. She tolerates my foibles, the worst of which are my sarcastic banter, my pernicious kidding of self-styled important people, and the earthy stories with which I enliven those exhausting sessions of the Church Board.

She lets me do things my way. Cooks my steaks and roasts rare. Always flatters me by asking me to carve the roast or fowl.

She is loyal to my family, and I to hers, although we pretend to argue furiously before the children about the in-law problem, always concluding with the profound deduction that "everyone has some half-baked relatives."

Mabel's patient, devoted care of my mother during her last years has its reward: a challenge to our own youngsters to share that same privilege equally and gladly when Mama gets "old and queer."

Mabel's robust father, past 81, whom our Robert, 12, calls a "great old boy," now shares our home in winter. This, frankly, involves some little sacrifices and muting of war-whoops and radios. But it's wholesome training for children who must learn that life involves adjusting to those who've helped us and now need us. (Grandpa in turn adjusts himself nobly—I sometimes wonder who is adjusting most!)

She is loyal to the church and persists—to our unholy irritation—in taking a seat up front, so that strangers and late-comers may have the more desirable back ones.

To her, participation is the essence of religion.

With a loud, clear voice, she takes off, a quarter-note sharp and a half-beat ahead of the new pipe organ, until that lesser and man-made vehicle of praise seems out of tune. Occasionally forgetting, in her enthusiasm, that *three* verses were announced, she takes off in full flight on verse *four*, just as the choir softly sings Amen. The young choristers smile, but Mabel, unabashed, winks and smiles back at them.

Meanwhile everybody is happy in the knowledge that after all, at no other home than ours are young people more welcome, nor does anyone else ever make any better—or more—cocoa for them.

To our own kids, and to all their pals, Mabel is symbolic of hospitality. Conscious that the church, the school, the home—yes, and the farm—are the four basic cornerstones of our society, she labors at each of them, exactly as she sings—always in full flight. (And I, the critic, cannot sing a note!)

She is a prodigious organizer of her energies, and has an "overdrive" that should be patented. But she has that rare faculty of complete and instant relaxation. She can lose herself in a book. She goes to and from the village library each week with a "Velveeta Cheese" box laden with well-chosen books for all of us. To our kids, "Kraft" must be the Patron Saint of Literature.

She is loyal to her friends, especially those whom she feels need her help. When she heard that the Rawleigh man was killed in a wreck, she said: "Oh, the poor man! Why didn't I buy two more bottles of vanilla, last week!"

I never saw anyone who hated sin so much, and could still be so darned nice to so many so-called sinners.

There was Florence, talented young woman whom the ugly serpent of scandal rose to devastate, perhaps unjustly. Mabel's reaction was instant and typical: "Florence has always been good to me. If she ever needed help she needs it now. I'm going up there with a quart of cream."

How that cream business of hers amuses us! She could sell it at the cream station for more than what she gets retailing and delivering it. But so many friends request our good Guernsey cream, safely pasteurized, that Mabel cannot refuse.

"Why," she says, indignantly, "Mrs. Jaspers is my very

best friend, and so poorly this summer. She's counting on my cream. I can't fail her now."

When death invades our community, Mabel's easy way of stepping into the situation with calm, assuring helpfulness makes her truly an angel of mercy. She is the kind that remembers to go back a week after the funeral, usually carrying cream, but always the milk of human kindness.

And I love her still, for her generosity. She will deny herself to assist a worthy cause, although this often borders on extravagance. One year she urged us to donate the several hundred dollars earmarked for our vacation to meet the church deficit. The five children and I, being the other members of the family council, agreed.

So we stayed home. That was the year the Bishop's family was sent on a vacation trip to India.

This year I almost wrote the Bishop to come help the boys and me wade through the steaming corn in August, pulling weeds, so that Mabel—bless her Methodist heart—could have the vacation she deserves!

Each Christmas finds her—with little regard for our bank account—remembering not so much the relatives, but the little tots around the town who still believe in Santa Claus, and who might just be overlooked.

She is generous with praise, too, which endears her to a lot of people who seldom hear praise. Come to think of it, that's just how she maneuvers *me* into doing the things she wants. Nagging doesn't work with me.

But I love her most of all for her glorious motherhood. Besides mothering our brood of four boys and one girl, I do believe she knows full names, ages, and epidemic histories of every other kid in the whole community. Our Eleanor, at six years, has her career picked out: "to be a Mama, just like Mama."

Mabel was a good cook long before she married me. Cooking for five growing kids has glorified her talent.

Each birthday merits an angel cake, with candles *et al,* and "Happy Birthday to yooo" rendered by the cockerel voices of our adolescent bassos.

Strange paradox peculiar to mothers: Mabel doesn't ask for love, but by the lavish spending of it, she has built a "life estate." She's both physician and psychologist, but better than a diploma, she has an understanding heart.

Wise in discipline, a job we share, she usually knows *when* and always knows *where* to spank.

When Robert or Harold had the croup—wherein a child can panic both himself and parents with his suffocation, always at an unearthly hour—Mabel held her fears so well in hand that the kids' sheer faith in her supplanted the doctor who was ten miles away.

Perhaps those lads later, in the black night of some embattled hillside, will hear in memory her words of faith, and know that somehow God—pinch-hitting for Mabel—will see them through until dawn.

A private word to you young husbands, who think you are so much in love. You're just barely sprouting! That love will have to send its roots deep down into the soil of worry and sorrow and sympathy and sacrifice.

The fairest petals of its bloom will be a row of diapers fluttering on the line, and you will grow ripe and sweet and mellow only after years of croup, and mumps, and adolescent romances have turned your hair to gray and the grandchildren begin to pull it out.

The other day I bought a lot in a cemetery that looks out on our homestead half a mile away. Alongside our lot are the neglected, unmarked graves of two infants. What a setup eventually for Mabel!

I can see her, hoisting a baby into each of her capable arms, making arrangements for them at the Gate. And God willing, I'll be close, loving her still.

—*Clarence S. Hill*

*L*ast year while preparing for our usual fairly extravagant Thanksgiving and thinking ahead to Christmas, I was haunted by a memory of this same season in a less plenteous time. I recalled Thanksgiving when I was 12. We'd had no guests and not a very big dinner. It was a day when nothing happened. Yet, years later, here I was remembering that particular day—poignantly.

In that first autumn of the Depression, the atmosphere we children had been brought up in had changed abruptly. We were a part of the economic collapse all about us, and our material future looked grim. Our family no longer took for granted the food available at mealtime, a half-

---

Suddenly life didn't seem lean or deprived. It was rich and sweet in a way I had never imagined.

---

ton of coal to give us heat, jackets on our backs against the wind. These were blessings for which we gave thanks. Our job was to try to maintain this basic sustenance.

The Thanksgiving nothing happened brought bleak weather without even the grace of snow to soften iron-frozen earth. But I was aglow—in a new dress Mother had made me from her store of fabrics. The dress was of bright blue silk and it had an intricately smocked yoke. Wearing it, I felt endowed with femininity as never before. With Eve I was one—and with my own mother.

That morning we rode our open-air Model T to church in the cutting wind. Standing in the pew among clusters of friends and neighbors—our companions in economic disaster—I heard my father's confident baritone above all other voices: *We gather together to ask the Lord's blessing....* Then something—a kind of awareness—tugged at me. Routine things became sharply significant: my father's singing of his faith in divine rightness; my mother's staying up nights to make my new dress.... Suddenly life didn't seem lean or deprived; it was rich and sweet in a way I had never imagined. In a crescendo of exaltation, I sensed my own destined role—in my parents' household, in the human family of continuing generations and in the house of the Lord.

A rather large and embracive emotion; but I was 12, remember.

I suppose my mother usually set a pretty table. However, this holiday I really *saw* a table that was beautiful to me: white cloth, bowl of red-fruited barberry branches. No turkey this year, but our small hen looked delicious on Mother's wedding-gift Haviland platter.

After the blessing we all talked, and my parents suddenly seemed to show a new, special respect for my conversation. I sensed in part what they were facing, and I was proud of their gallantry. The curtains had parted; I had taken my first step into the community of privileges and obligations of adult life. Uncertainty was our silent guest; but I was certain, with my parents, that love—and living life with dignity—was what really mattered.

All this was long ago. Remembering, amid my now ample existence, I was illogically wistful for those bad times. I longed for the atmosphere that encouraged an appreciation of the essentials, a sensitivity to life, a receptiveness to its disciplines and rewards. I reflected that in our modern, plentiful era, children have little chance to learn—and we older folks seldom pause to remember—the values that emerge and abide best in adversity. We don't really appreciate the important things we have; and too often the fluff of life takes first place. Material good fortune has stifled growth of the spirit.

I fell to coveting my own early experience for my children. I feared they would never know that richness I had awakened to in a different time and culture, that year when I was 12.

I was in this mood when seventh-grade Steve came tearing off the school bus to begin Christmas holidays. This was at noon, four days before the Day. We weren't yet into the last-minute rush; and since my every day ordinarily belongs to our pre-school Mary, I planned to give Steve special holiday attention this afternoon. We could see a movie, have one of his friends in, or aisle-shop the new discount department store on the highway.

Steve is 12. But he is not like me at the same age. Steve is busy with many activities, he has many things. His days are organized into educational and pleasurable affairs. Like other modern children, he takes these "advantages" casually. He does his chores casually, too—because he's supposed to, and not because of any compulsion to make a contribution to the family.

When he hustled in, I began enumerating possibilities of fun for the afternoon. Thoughtfully he considered my "Would you like to?" suggestions. Finally he said, "No. Let's just fool around."

So, fooling around, Steve shaped the afternoon. Out on the porch he sawed and tailored the Christmas tree to living room space. Then he erected it, anchored it, covered the base with a white sheet. With patience and authority usually missing, he allowed small Mary to help him string lights, hang ornaments, drape strings of beads and tinsel.

The tree done, he shoved Mary's feet into her galoshes so she could follow him in the woods while he cut some greens. With these he festooned our rooms. The blue angel, the tiny creche and a few mobile stars went into their places on and about the mantel.

By now it was dark. The fire was lit; supper was ready. The glad bark of Fritz, our German Shepherd, announced that husband Jim was home. The day was almost ended. A pleasant day, but one of routine holiday chores. A day on which nothing had happened.

We gathered around the table, asking the blessing. I tuned the radio higher so we could hear carols. We were eating by candlelight—"Can everyone see?" I asked fussbudgetly.

Steve was quiet a long moment (often I'm not sure whether or not he has heard me). Finally he said—wonderingly, as if he'd made a discovery: "It's beautiful." Then, gently, "Mother, I've just loved this day. It's been the best day of my life."

His soft observation shook my cynicism back a full generation. Here again was that precious 12-year-old feeling—a wonderful, sensitive awareness—in my son.

Yes, it can happen at Thanksgiving, or at Christmas, or on just any day. In good times or bad, the values that guide us humans reappear in each successive generation. As your boy or girl, in due time, reaches that day when the deeper meanings of life start to unfold, you may relive such a time yourself—a day when nothing much happened, yet everything seemed to begin.

—*Virginia Brown Rose*

PLACE OF QUIETNESS

A barn can be a place of quietness.
The rafters, lifting up cathedral high,
Arch overhead. Space muffles and hushes
Voice or footsteps. Dimness rests the eye.
A pigeon coos, and from the vaulted roof
As from an organ, gentle echoes sound
A stable was a Birthplace, long ago.
And in all barns a quietness is found.
      Mildred Goff

*U*ntil I had a long illness, I prided myself on being independent. "Do it yourself," was my motto.

Such foolish pride! But I came by it naturally. My grandmother used to say, "Don't be beholden to anyone!"

Then I found myself helpless and in need of someone to "do" for me.

Two friends who were nurses' aides offered to take turns giving me a bed-bath every day. Of course I refused! Both were busy homemakers. Take all that time to come in and give me a bath? "No!" Definitely "No!"

My friends looked at each other, and I saw the light go from their faces. They were disappointed. They *wanted* to

---

I found myself helpless and in need of someone.

---

give me this gift of themselves, and I was depriving them of the joy of giving.

The next day I sent word to each one. "I've changed my mind," I told them. "Please do help me."

So for weeks, Marion's or Lois' pleasant face would appear at my bedroom door each morning and I would bask gratefully in the enjoyment of having loving, tender hands take care of me. It was beautiful to see their happiness in giving—happiness I had so nearly spoiled.

This set me thinking about how necessary it is for us to receive as well as to give. Most of us find giving pleasant and easy. We enjoy remembering friends and relatives at Christmas, giving to the March of Dimes, lavishing time and energy on neighborhood and community. We have been brought up in the Christian philosophy that is is "more blessed to give than to receive."

Yet Jesus received Martha's loving ministrations gratefully, and when He sent His disciples forth He commanded them, "Take nothing for your journey, neither staves, nor scrip, neither bread, neither money. . . ." He wanted them to be on the receiving end so that others might know the pleasure of service.

Receiving from family and friends shouldn't be difficult—because they love you. It is not so easy to accept favors and gifts from mere acquaintances or total strangers. Yet, that is the kind of receiving which builds the brotherhood of man.

Last Christmas, on a farm home in New York State, a Christmas tree caught fire just as a family (father, mother, and four small children) began opening presents. The family escaped safely, but everything in the room was ruined—tree, presents, furniture.

Neighbors came to help, and by noon they had cleaned the walls of soot, put down a rug, carried in tables and chairs, put up a small tree and under it heaped gifts from their own Christmas treasure.

How grateful the family was! The father kept repeating "I just don't know how to pay you back for your wonderful kindness!"

I hope he won't try. I'm sure the pleasure of giving was repayment enough. A feeling of gratitude will warm that man's heart for the remainder of his life whenever he thinks of that Christmas—just as I cherish the thought of the un-pay-backable gift from Lois and Marion. The only way to express our gratitude is to pass on such kindness through help to others.

A mother whom I know cannot receive—*she* must always be the one to give. So, she spoils her daughter, Margaret. She washes and irons Margaret's clothes, makes fancy desserts for Margaret's friends to eat, and won't even let this teen-age girl make her own bed! Now she is beginning to complain that Margaret doesn't appreciate how hard she works, yet she refuses Margaret's offers of help. No, she can do a task in less time than it will take to show Margaret how. . . . So both mother and child are losing the richness of living that comes through a balance between giving and receiving.

How often rifts occur between in-laws because one side or the other refuses to be a gracious *receiver*. Recently a bride came to me in tears, asking for advice. She and her husband had just returned from visiting his family. Anne was eager for her mother-in-law to like her, and when the first mealtime together came around, she went to the kitchen and offered to help.

"Oh, no," was the reply, "it would make me nervous. I can do it faster myself."

Anne, subdued and chilled, asked her husband what she should do. "I don't want your mother to feel burdened because we're here."

"Let's do the dishes for her," he suggested.

But that plan had to be given up after a few trials. The mother complained that they were careless and that they really made more work for her in the end. The bride and groom did not stay long! If only the mother had been able to receive, how close she and her daughter-in-law might have grown.

A poor receiver not only deprives others of the happiness of giving but loses the joy of knowing that someone cares enough to want to give.

When you stop saying "I'll be beholden to no one," and learn to accept graciously, new understanding will glow warmly in your heart.

Mary G. Phillips

OLD RECIPE BOOK

*This brings my Mother closer to me
    now
Than pen or portrait—just this faded
    book.
Only ingredients are listed here: not
    how
To mix them. I can see her reproach-
    ful look:
"Why, you remember that, my child,
    for certain!"
I can hear her saying: "That one is
    from Mabel!"
I recall sun shifting through a ging-
    ham curtain
Making a stained-glass cover for the
    table.
I use these recipes now over and over:
Fat biscuit, shortcake, and top-heavy
    loaves
Of golden-crusted bread as sweet as
    clover,
And when the scent of cinnamon and
    cloves
Spice the warm air, those days return
    once more,
And memory consecrates each homely
    chore.*

                Eleanor Alletta Chaffee

A drizzling rain that morning eleven years ago made it hard for my sister-in-law to drive. But for me, sitting beside her, the world was rose-tinged. I was 25, in superb health and in love with my husband. We had a citrus grove and two small children, and were happily expecting our third baby.

It took only a split second—the skid of our car across the wet highway and a crash into a culvert—to change my life as completely as if I had entered another world.

The impact threw me out in the ditch on the back of my neck. My feet were trapped in the car and rain pelted down in my face. There was a searing pain across my shoulders; I could hear the windshield wiper swishing back and forth. . . .

Later at the hospital, I learned that my neck was broken.

Finally two men came along. They covered us gently, with some bedspreads we had shopped for that morning and had in the car. Then, obviously shaken by our plight—one woman unconscious, the other eight months pregnant and hanging by her feet from a wrecked car—they went for help.

My sister-in-law stirred and sat up by the time an ambulance arrived. She was dazed but not seriously hurt. I could not move. Later at the hospital, I learned that my neck was broken. My husband sat with me, white and stunned, in the ambulance that took me on to a larger hospital where specialists were available.

The doctors decided they would have to take my baby in an effort to save its life. Saving mine looked doubtful. By the time I was prepared for surgery, I was hardly breathing. I heard a nurse say, "She'll never make it," and her words filled me with fury such as I had never known. I'd show her. I *would* live!

I came through the Caesarean to learn that we had another healthy son; but I could not hold him, nor pick him up nor change him. My head had been shaved so that surgical instruments could be attached; to soften the starkness I asked nurses to Scotch-tape a ribbon bow to my pate. This, to the hospital staff, became my badge of courage. For me it was a note of brightness in a world gray with helplessness and anxiety.

Motionless, and in traction for three months, I could see nothing of the outside world except the very tip of a palm frond that blew back and forth across my line of vision. The doctors did their best to encourage me; but I had shown almost no progress when, about five months after the accident, they let me go home in an ambulance.

I had forgotten how beautiful the world was outside of hospital walls. With heightened awareness, I drank in the colors, the sunshine and shadows, sounds and smells. I could not look enough at my family. I wanted to hold my children close, but could not.

Weeks of therapy followed, and agonizing effort on my part to move even my arms. There were endless X-rays, tests, explorations, consultations. On the long-awaited day of my checkup I went cheerfully to the doctor's office, anticipating a hopeful report.

But as the doctor picked up one of my useless hands, I looked quickly at his face and saw defeat written there. I knew then that I would use neither my arms nor legs as long as I lived. Never again would I brush my little daughter's silky hair, nor wash my sons' ears, nor make love with my husband, nor keep a house nor cook.

Terror possessed me and despair rode hard on its heels. Our savings were gone and we were thousands of dollars in debt. How could any family survive such a burden, plus the constantly escalating expenses of caring for an invalid? How could our children's lives be anything but tragic? How could my husband carry his triple burden—make a living, rear three small children and look after a hopeless paralytic?

Finally, from beneath my morass of shattered hopes and broken body, that thin tendril of fighting spirit emerged again, and it would not be denied. With astonishment I realized that I still wanted to live, even with in-

---

With astonishment, I realized
I still wanted to live.
The battle ahead was not one
for a weakling.

---

surmountable odds. I could not bear to think of leaving my family.

So, painfully, I took stock. My mentality, speech and four of the five senses—sight, hearing, taste and smell—were unimpaired. Could I, though bedfast, again make a home for my husband and children? The battle ahead was not one for a weakling.

I started with discipline, mainly of myself. Self-pity had to go and I must come to terms with fear. I must stop agonizing over how long my husband could stand such an existence. I must adjust to not being able to go places with him, to being shut off from physical closeness. I must rid myself of resentment over his occasional evenings out. (Reason told me that these were necessary to replenish his spirit, if not to save his sanity; but emotionally I anguished.)

I must, although paralyzed, be a person my children could be proud of. Moreover, I must discipline them as well as myself. I must get it over to them that I was in complete charge and not to be disobeyed. This wasn't easy, since all three were, and are, normal, healthy youngsters. But to their credit, not one of them has ever run away from me to escape an edict or verbal punishment.

To keep me familiar with the house, my husband gave me wheelchair tours. I memorized the placement of furniture, the contents of drawers, the clothing in each closet. Then woe to anyone who put anything in a wrong place!

It took some doing to keep in mind our grocery inventory, to plan meals and make complete lists for my husband's once-a-week shopping expeditions.

We do have problems; one of our most serious is housekeepers. We must have one, and obviously a housekeeper working for us has no easy lot. By the time I get one trained, she may leave for more money or less responsibility. The upheaval and confusion of training and re-training upset us terribly.

How adversity can change one's values! A few years ago, I was much concerned with material things—an impressive home and car, the best of clothes. I still like nice things; but, more important, I know a spiritual and emotional fullness that no amount of material possessions could bring. Once I took life and health for granted. I even complained of too much to do. Now, for life itself I am wholeheartedly grateful. I thank God that I am freed from bitterness; that my family and I share a genuine closeness. I can even value my husband's evenings out, knowing he will bring some of the world back to me.

Our family enjoyments take an inordinate lot of managing. The success of our plan will hinge on whether I am up to an outing on the appointed day. But oh, the pleasure when we do manage one of our rare picnics!

To say that I am proud of our children is an understatement. They accept responsibility far beyond their years, even financial (they've all started savings accounts from cash gifts on birthdays and Christmases). Each does well in school and knows that he will have to work for his college education.

My children's gifts to me are compassion, love and an almost selfless serving. In return I try to set an example of courage and perseverence. Perhaps more important, my husband and I let the children know that we value them and appreciate their help.

Sometimes I get impatient—to get the children reared, to pay all the debts; for how long can our miracle last? But one great truth I have learned. Each day is a rare jewel, to be treasured and lived to the fullest.

I no longer think primarily of five years from now, or two or even one. My hope always is to be granted the priceless gift of another tomorrow.

—*Irene Williams,* as told to Joyce L. Hutchinson

THE COLLECTORS

"Do you collect arrowheads?" the lady asked,
"Or butterflies, or music, or cooking
*   recipes or what?"*
Shall I tell her we collect happy days—
Finding them, sometimes, without looking?
We may come upon one as perfect as an
Arrowhead, or as glowing as Monarch wings,
Or as lilting as Rubenstein's Melody in F.
Sometimes a day is like a recipe for which
We supply work needing to be done, and rest,
Patience, understanding, and the best
Laughter available, good talk, and the most
Important ingredient: love.
Will she think that I exaggerate?
                    Elaine V. Emans

*I*t was five days after my husband's surgery when I drove over to Rim Farm—our place that looks over into Snake River Canyon—to cut thistles. My spirits were as low as the wilting brambles that fell at my feet. I bent over the spade, feeling the heat of the noon sun upon my back.

I was thinking, why must bad luck always come in one big, smothering wave? For Vaughn and me, anyway! Our bean fields had been blackened by early frost last fall; we'd had to borrow more money to finance spring plant-

---

Why must bad luck always come in one big, smothering wave?

---

ing. Our son had sailed for Vietnam and our faithful old dog had died. The gophers were digging in the ditches, playing havoc with the irrigation water. . . . And that morning in the hospital Vaughn had said despondently: "Honey, I'll never lift another shovel."

Anyway, I thought firmly, I could cut these Canadian thistles. They were growing like crazy. I looked at the beads of sweat on the backs of my hands, felt the drops slither down my back. I had reassured Vaughn, "You are going to be fine"—well knowing that having two-thirds of his stomach removed could weaken a man for life. "Meanwhile," I had said brightly, "I am going to the Rim and cut some thistles." ·

Vaughn had smiled thinly. "Be sure to cut the mortgaged ones." (Were there any other kinds?)

I worked steadily for two hours—to music, courtesy of a meadowlark. I glimpsed the lark's yellow feathers, and a butterfly echoed that brilliant color. ·

Rim Farm has special fragrances in summer: pungent sage, greening grasses and wheat shoots. The waterfall roared in my ears as it tumbled over the canyon wall. "Guess I'll do some irrigating," I said aloud.

I drove the pickup over to the new seeding of bluegrass. Here the water rippled along in a rocky ditch. I dropped the wooden gate as I'd seen Vaughn do so many times, and watched the water spread across the thirsty field. There were more thistles along the ditch. . . .

At the hospital that afternoon, one of Vaughn's nurses said to me, "You look different—more relaxed. What's your tranquilizer?" When I told her "thistles," she looked at me a little strangely, I thought.

Vaughn walked stooped-over when he came home from the hospital. July dragged along through the intense heat. I mowed the lawn, weeded the tomatoes, hung sheets out to dry, washed windows, wrote letters . . . and in between such chores, I'd get back to work on those thistles.

Finally the day came when a coolness was in the west wind and autumn crickets started to sing. There was a change in my husband, too. He ate a hearty breakfast and said, "That old cistern's caved in. I'm going to fill it up with dirt."

I gasped, "You'll fill it? I thought you couldn't handle a shovel any more!"

"Come and see," he challenged.

So I did, and watched Vaughn's shovel move as easily as a fork lifting mashed potatoes.

At the Rim I cut thistles with new vigor. The spade seemed not so heavy now. I paused a moment to enjoy the goldenrod modeling its plumage against our dark lava rocks. The waterfall had lowered its roar to a murmur—another sound of autumn.

There had been no frost. The bean crop was good and harvest would soon be under way. This promised money to pay the hospital bill and the bank loan. We had heard from our Navy son; he would be home for Christmas! He would enjoy our new dog as we do; she romps about in the hayfield and falls in the ditch while digging for gophers, just like old Buttons used to do.

Life had not stopped just because big trouble came. The seasons were still rolling along and the good earth still produced for us. I felt a surge of energy as the noon sun laid a warm hand on my back. I realized that I had been doing more than cut thistles out of the fields all summer; I'd also been cutting them out of my mind. With the thistles of self-pity, doubt and worry no longer choking my mind, there was room for optimism to grow.

Vaughn came down the lane carrying a scythe. "I'll help," he called. I stopped to admire the easy rhythm with which he swung the scythe. He wiped the sweat from his forehead. "Honey, someday there won't be any more mortgaged thistles to cut," he declared.

I'd miss them, I knew suddenly. I would always need a few thistles to work on—when I'd get to worrying about our son, or that Vaughn's ulcer might come back, or that bean blight might threaten again. . . .

So now, though I cut the really big weeds, I leave a few of the smaller ones to grow. It's best to be prepared.

Elsie D. Hunt

The Rewarding Years

PONDERING AND RESOLUTION

Request

Give me as I grow old, to bless my days,
Not alone a wish, a faith fulfilled,
Not alone a longing quenched or stilled;
The heart has other needs, joy other ways.
Give me instead some problem to be solved,
A song unfinished, a design undone,
Some pattern to complete, some work begun
Whatever challenges may be involved.
New plans half formed—how I shall welcome
    these:
A rising hope, a stripling dream outcast
But building still—and, Lord, if You would
    please
Me most of all, then give me, toward the last,
A pocketful of seed and the strength for sowing,
And a fallow field, a child near, and a young
    tree growing!

Helen Harrington

*M*any people, I suppose, go to the Memorial Day parade for the wrong reasons—son Andrew plays in the band, or he has a crush on a girl whom he hopes to encounter, Ma wants to see what the Firemen's Auxiliary did with the float. My persuasions are likewise more inclined to stir the body than the soul.

"Can't we go to the parade, Ma? Everybody else is going. You're not doin' anything important"—my boys put on the pressure. Well, someone made the effort to take me to parades when I was a kid and I feel a sense of obligation. It has seemed nice to have a day with "nothing important," but reluctantly I submit.

Many people, I suppose
go to the Memorial Day Parade
for the wrong reasons . . . .

The mood is relaxed and gay. The parade is gathering in the school yard. Somebody's hawking balloons, and a civic group is doing a land office business in candy and popcorn. Teen-agers find their buddies and sit in parked cars where radios drown out the silence between them.

All along the parade route friends greet and form clusters of spectators. Residents with porches know the annual pride of a house with a view and call to passing acquaintances to bring up their folding chairs. Children fight and chase and wheedle.

Finally the whistle, the muffled drum beat. The little kids scurry back to their places on the curb and the longest minutes of the waiting, then the parade.

The convertible passes with the mayor and the minister

who will give the oration. The band zeroes in on a march; the acquaintance next to me fills the conversational gap with, "They certainly sound good for a high school band, don't they?" Before I can agree (or disagree) they are upon us, and that old cornball lump that I have for flags, anthems, alma maters, and suffering or rejoicing humanity chokes me off. A good friend runs by with his camera trying to get a bead on Andrew and restores me to objective spectator.

I enjoy with some nostalgia the Legionnaires in their slightly snug uniforms; I remember most of them as high school heroes. Then passes Old Glory done by the Grange—a magnificent feat in Kleenex, crepe paper and chicken wire. The volunteer firemen over a case of beer have done their best by the brass and chrome on their equipment and ride past in high happy state. There are visiting corps of lumpy little majorettes in over-priced costumes led by their instructors, who are lovelier and shapelier. The Scouts troop by, a women's drill team, a few more floats, a couple of antique cars, and the bicycles wound in red, white and blue bunting. Toward the end come the horses (pridefully groomed from teeth to tail) and straining for the freedom of pastures to which they are more accustomed. In the rear, looking unrelated to the body of the parade, are a couple of kids with hot rods, only slightly less groomed than the horses.

But somehow I am not "with it." I am a cynic watching a parade. I only see people celebrating themselves. What has all this to do with memorializing? Something on this day eludes me. . . .

We tail the parade through the cemetery gates and take a place on the grass. More band music, a hush in the crowd, *The Star-Spangled Banner*, and my lump is back. The mayor introduces the minister who starts his oration.

I follow him for few sentences; then I find myself thinking of "Mutz," our basketball star of a long ago winter who went down on a ship in the Pacific; of Hank who died on a battlefield in France trying to help a wounded buddy; of Peter, smiling, warm, wonderful Pete, who crashed with his air crew over Korea; of John, affable, capable, questioning John who gave his life in a Vietnamese jungle. I think of the uncle I never knew who marched blithely off to the strains of *Over There* and met his Armageddon in the trenches of Lorraine.

Did they go for the wrong reasons, reluctantly, as I came today? Was it escape? Glory? Or an incomprehensible yielding to an indefinable duty?

The orator has finished; the Legionnaires march into po-si-shun! and taps is sounding. Somewhere behind an evergreen Andrew muffs a note. Tears squeeze from my eyes and roll down alongside my nose.

The mayor and the speaker walk back to the car; the band beats a quick tempo to the gate and disbands. People pick up their blankets and make their way out, stopping to exchange the incessant small talk. The little boys are pulling at me, teasing to go back and buy balloons. I wish that everyone would go quietly away and leave me there in the cemetery with my thoughts.

Why did they die, Mutz, Pete, John, Uncle Jack, the thousands of others? So that someone could sit in a cemetery and weep? Certainly not for that.

When life finally became serious for these young men, when they faced their "rendezvous with death," what reasons did they find? Were they, as we choose to hope, motivated by a dream of worldwide freedom and fulfillment of the individual? And what did freedom and fulfillment mean to them? Is not this the sort of day they remembered when they wanted to obliterate the hell of war?

These men were young, and their concern was living. If they had to die for something, why not for this—so that a farm kid could get into town to see his girl and buy a hot dog; so that Ma could forget her problems when she practiced with a drill team; so the fellows at the firehouse could have a few beers together on a holiday; so a pretty young thing could earn money for a trousseau by coaching young majorettes; so the Scout could march and the parents watch; so a kid could have a hot rod and shine it for a special occasion? These are the casual preoccupations of a free people. This is "living" for the sort of young men who die in battle; this is freedom and all the fulfillment most of them ever knew.

Who am I to judge whether they died for the wrong reasons?

Who am I, for that matter, to say that I came to town today for the wrong reasons? Yes, let's go back to the school and buy balloons—lots of them. And I'll watch them float out over the playground—one for Mutz, one for Hank, one for Pete, one for John, one for my doughboy uncle, and one for every other soldier who would have chosen to be here today buying balloons for his son, his grandson, his kid brother, or his girl friend, if he hadn't died somewhere for "freedom for all men."

—*Patricia Penton Leimbach*

NONSENSE SHARED

I don't remember ever laughing as a child. It was my husband who taught me—and our children—how a little silliness can lighten the heart.
   Texas homemaker

231

I wish you a Merry Christmas! Such simple words. And for each person who says them there is probably a different meaning—according to the kind of growing up he had, the pattern of his present life and facets of his unique personality. If we moderns approached Christmas more reflectively—took more time for soul-searching—I would like to stop those who greet me with a "Merry Christmas," clutch them by the arm, look into their eyes and say, "What do you mean by that?" And if someone else should stop me with such a question, I am at least partially ready with my answer:

"Merry Christmas!" *"What do you mean by that?"*

My friend, I wish you good health and peace of mind. May you look upon life with optimism and good cheer, even in a world that insists on fomenting violence, hatred and war. May you have an indestructible faith, to survive today's incredible griefs, separations, confusions. And a questioning mind: *What is my stake in Peace on Earth? What is my part in helping to fulfill the Promise?*

I wish you to have the fragrances of cedar and oranges, nutmeg and cinnamon and bayberry candles. I would that you should have lights of some kind in your house after dark—the varicolored, winking lights of your Christmas tree, or a candle in the window—so that others can see that you are there and that all is well with you.

May you have some family around you, and especially some children with sparkle in their eyes as you tell them the story of Bethlehem's manger. . . . I wish for you some gifts to give, and joy in the giving.

May you stand in starlit silence and hear the angels sing. I hope you'll hear bells, too—church bells chiming their silver notes, street-corner bells asking you to share with "the least of these," sleigh bells, doorbells. . . . You must also hear carols old and new, and join in the singing. May you have a fat goose or a turkey and all the other goodies, rich memories of Christmases past. . . . And would you mind a little snow? Just a little, falling at tender, blue-shadowy twilight time.

But most of all I wish you some solitude wherein you can let your mind drift back over the centuries, to that special night when God became man and lived amongst us for a while. May you go with the shepherds or the Wise Men to that little Judaean town of Micah's prophecy and in your heart be near to the One who was to say, "My peace I give unto you . . . I will not leave you comfortless . . . be of good cheer."

—*Jean Bell Mosley*

*W*hen my world becomes a dizzy round of perpetual motion filled with demands that sharpen my tongue, or when self-pity nibbles at my spirit, I "go sit on a rock." After an hour or so my whole state of mind rearranges itself into a more harmonious pattern, and I'm comfortable with myself again.

I do not understand how this miracle happens. But in the quietness of rock-sitting, the way ahead becomes more clear, my cares grow lighter and that will-o'-the-wisp Happiness does not seem so elusive.

"Rock-sitting" begins early in life. All children have an innate need of a place for solitary reflection. Every one of us can remember such a spot—an attic, a corner, a grape arbor, a haymow, a fencerow, or a willow tree whose dripping branches walled in a room without windows. These were our private retreats where oldsters did not penetrate, and where there was quiet enough for dreams to sprout and grow.

Each escape spot was a haven where we could retire to lick our imagined or real wounds after a lost bout in the adult world. In those early years we did not realize that

After an hour or so of rock-sitting, I'm comfortable with myself again.

even grownups often can't find a sense of reason in their world; that they, also, need a place to sit down and sort out their problems and confusions.

I have a special rock that I call mine although I am not its deed owner. It heads a deep gully and is worn smooth by all the life that goes on above it. This hard psychiatric couch is the right size for sitting, and the sun nearly always finds it.

In March it is the only warm spot in a cold world. Sitting here, I can see the first anemones finding their way through the winter moss and hear a frog's initial quaver from the marshes. I am reminded that frogs made the lonely sound a Pharaoh listened to as it arose, strident and harsh, from the Nile. My rock is only a short distance from a busy highway, but I seem to be in a wilderness where time is a slow, natural process rather than a pressure system.

April builds a new world here; the sun lingers, drugging warm, in the hollows: it stencils shadows of the budding trees against my rain-washed rock. On a July day the rock is a shaded pinnacle where I can rest at the end of woods-wandering. If I am very quiet, a few birds gather to serenade me; a curious squirrel may whisk close enough to question my inertia.

I have sat on my rock in the fall, when the shadows on it seem to reflect the rich autumn colors from the surrounding foliage. Scarcely breathing, I can hear the dried leaves skitter by. There is a melancholy note in rock-sitting then, as I try to store up enough peace to last the winter.

In this hurried pace we call modern living, I recommend rock-sitting to regain your perspective. It's a time-tested therapy, and inexpensive, and even the busiest person can steal a while to enjoy it. If you "go sit on a rock" for just one hour, you will experience a little of the miracle.

—*Helen Virden*

When we sit beneath a spot-lighted cross on Good Friday and listen to the stirring hymns of the passion and death of Jesus, the experience becomes for many an emotional cleansing. I know the feeling, having come away often with tears in my throat, feeling somehow ready for the reward of Easter morning.

Yet the mounting anguish of our nation and the world in the events of the year past convince me that Christians can no longer limit themselves to this obsession with the tragedy of the historic Jesus. The suffering Christ must be seen as the symbol of a suffering humanity throughout the world—today.

It is my conviction that on Good Friday we must look for the faces on the cross in our time, and search ourselves for the compassion necessary to identify with them.

As a mother, I inevitably come to Good Friday looking through a mother's eyes, but I shall not try as usual this year to regain the feeling of Mary as she saw her beloved son "despised" and watched him die on the cross.

I shall try instead to imagine what it is to be the mother of a crippled, retarded, or disadvantaged child, who is despised in a strange way for not being "normal." Surely there is crucifixion in seeing your own child rejected.

I shall weep for the mothers of sons killed by other

I come to Good Friday looking through a mother's eyes.

---

mothers' sons carefully taught to despise in the hell of war. I shall try to imagine the suffering of war's innocents left hungry, homeless, bereaved—crucified in conflicts unchecked by a society that can produce life in a test tube and orbit the moon. War is a continuous crucifixion.

I shall kneel in sorrow this Good Friday for the thousands of unloved children born yearly, for Godless masses, bitter and despised, growing into another alienated generation which may carry out crucifixions of their own.

On the cross this year I shall see the joyless faces of the young, lost in limbo between their parents' past-generation values and their own, not yet formed.

But overlying all these will be a collage of individuals who struggle to halt these crucifixions in their separate spheres of human influence (some have died in the effort, even this year). I will look for my place in my sphere—and I will go beyond Good Friday to Easter. Not, as always, seeking hope for myself in Resurrection, but with hope of resurrection for the people who hang on Good Friday's crosses.

I will pray that Easter may bring a rededication of the advantaged to the causes of the alienated, the afflicted, the unloved. And with me all the while will be the disturbing certainty that if we do not find compassion in our hearts for today's crucified, there may come a Good Friday when we shall find ourselves among the crucified.

—Patricia Penton Leimbach

My husband has been gone seven years now. It has taken me this long to sort out my thoughts and to have the spirit to bring them out in the open. Even now, this isn't easy. I do it only because I now understand what a shattering experience being left a widow has been to many women—and will be to many of you.

"But you were such a self-sufficient person," my friends say to me. "You traveled all over the world when you were president of The Associated Country Women of the World. You have so many friends and interests."

Yes, I do. But if any widow ever felt more keenly alone, and desolate, I pity her. Until you yourself have been through this most devastating experience, it is hard to imagine what it is like.

For suddenly part of you is gone. It is a drastic severance—as real as if you had lost a part of your own self—an arm or a leg. Now you must literally learn to walk again—alone. Even the most independent of us have become more dependent than we know. You feel small, timid, uncertain. Once so sure of yourself, so able to make decisions, you are now unsure, lost.

It means the loss of companionship—someone to talk everything over with, someone who is "always there." It means that your life has suddenly lost its direction and purpose. How can you go on? What is the use?

"Widow"—most unhappy word!
For the first time, I really
understood the meaning of the
words "till death do us part."

"Widow"—most unhappy word! I had never thought of applying it to myself. For the first time I really understood the meaning of the words "till death do us part." I was no longer married! Now I must learn to say "I" instead of "we," "mine" not "ours."

My own first reaction was—why did it have to happen? My husband was badly hurt when a tree fell on him on our own farm, but it was a blood clot a few days later that stopped his heart. I questioned the competence of the doctor: Why hadn't he given more anti-clotting drug . . . had he really done all he could?

Even my faith underwent a bitter test. My husband loved life to the full and had much to live for. Why should

238

God take him so soon? Why, why, why? I questioned the whole of life and the hereafter as I had never questioned them before. Meanwhile, I knew that I had to work out some philosophy with which I could learn to live without bitterness and self-pity.

I finally came to feel that my husband's death was not God-designed—that God's design is for goodness.

You have to accept that it isn't God-against-me when something like this happens, but that death is part of the pattern of life. We can't expect to remain untouched. Because I am a farm woman and have lived for so many years with the laws of Nature's seasons, I believe it was a little easier for me to accept this.

We farm women know everything "dies"—I wonder whether it wouldn't help us to say everything "changes" instead. We have come to think of death as an ending, while actually the spirit of a person lives on with us and contributes to our lives after death. Just as a plant plowed under nurtures new plants that nurture new plants . . . and so on.

My husband's death made me think more about religion . . . what is "eternity"? . . . Going through this shattering experience makes you less apt to accept other people's religion, even the minister's. But the religion you come out with means more to you. So though I started out with bitterness, I grew in my inner life.

I found that I had to build a completely new life in other ways too. The biggest mistake widows can make, I've decided, is not to understand and accept that their lives will be changed. I'm afraid most women make this silent emotional pledge to the absent one: I will "carry on" the same way we always did. (I felt that way at first.) I'm convinced that is exactly what a woman shouldn't do. You won't start getting emotionally healed until you accept that nothing will ever be the same again.

Instead, I found that you have to build a new life. Otherwise you will live the rest of your life with a feeling of unhappiness, uselessness and self-pity. It isn't easy, as I know so well.

First, do take time to make any decisions about the future. For me, it seemed best to stay where I was—on the farm in the home we had made together. In the panic that follows the loss of the person she leaned on, many a farm woman promises to move near her sister, to sell or rent her place. My advice is: If you can, wait, because such a drastic change may be wrong for you.

I'm glad I stayed on the farm. Of course, I was more fortunate than many women—my son lived on an adjoining place and we could enter into a partnership. But I live alone in our farmhouse and I wouldn't have it any other way. All my roots are there and in my garden, which has helped me.

I admit I felt differently about the house at first. It was easy to say: Why bother to paint the living room or get a new screen door . . . I'm just here alone. But keeping your home attractive for your children and friends will give purpose to your life—gradually this will again do things for you, too.

Many people wondered why I stayed on the farm and in a small community. I have a daughter in Washington, D.C., and I like to travel and see far places. But my community, too, was part of me—it was something comfortable to fall back on. People knew me; they understood my problems; they made no big demands on me.

I could retreat to work out my thoughts, but I had good friends and neighbors. And let no one tell you that old friends aren't the best at a time like this—they are. Just the same, you must learn to live with loneliness.

At a time when you most need the person to whom you can say anything because he understands you so well, you don't have that person. I think it is the loneliest feeling in the world.

Often it's the little things that hit you hardest. I couldn't face going to shop for groceries, for example—my husband and I had always done that together.

I moved around in a world that seemed suddenly inhabited only by couples. You *will* be left out when your status changes back to singleness. Not consciously, perhaps, but just by the nature of our society. And it will hurt. It is a little strange that our society, built on the worth of the individual, has such a couple complex.

I'm glad I stayed on the farm. All my roots are there.

Of course, if you have been a working wife and have a job, you are fortunate. The routine of a job would have been a godsend to me.

The easiest way, if you have children, is to lean on them. And I'm afraid many women take out their bitterness and loneliness on their children and make their lives unhappy. How a woman has to resist this temptation! It can so easily become a habit.

It is as hard for me as for any mother to let go of her children and let them live their own lives. Especially when I so often think I know better what's best for them! But I work hard at this.

What do I do? I keep busy! You may catch me doing needlepoint. (I never did needlepoint before in my life.) I'm piecing quilts. (Never did that before either.) With calico scraps from my mother's and my husband's mother's attics, I am making "heritage" quilts.

I find that much of my busyness has to do with my children, and their lives after I shall be gone. For instance, I've had a real binge of cleaning out and throwing away—I'm not going to leave my children the burden of going through years of accumulations in attics.

But I am keeping the things that will be of real interest. I am making scrapbooks for my children of their father's and my activities. I am digging back in our family history as far as I can. This has even led me to visiting old churches in England to examine family records. It is a rewarding kind of heritage to leave, I feel. Roots are good to have. Strong, long roots, as any farm woman knows.

Many of my friends wonder why, for someone who had responsibilities in organizations, I did not "forget myself" in activities. Well, it so happened that my husband's death came when I had just finished my term as President of ACWW and the travel to other countries that it involved.

I was looking forward to more time with him at home, to trips we would take together. Suddenly, I was without responsibilities that had kept me unusually busy and "needed." Just when my husband's death left a terrible vacuum, I wasn't needed anywhere, it seemed.

The habits of a lifetime now came to my rescue. I read and read during many a wakeful night—stories of Queen Victoria and Martha Washington and how they—as women—met this same crisis.

I still kept on traveling—to the Middle East with friends one year; around the world alone another time; at the invitation of good friends a trip through New England in the fall, including antiquing—one of my hobbies. I spent many hours writing letters to friends at home and around the world.

I turned to local things, which I had not had time for during the busy years—the cancer drive, garden club, the nearby art center. But even in these activities I sat back; I had preached for so long that young people should have their chance for leadership, that now I had to practice it.

I accepted new responsibilities in promoting safety. Because an accident caused my husband's death, my safety work took on new meaning. These things helped to push back the dark loneliness.

Since we cannot choose the time when death enters our lives—and since statistics prove that many of you farm women will outlive your husbands—it seems to me we

---

The biggest mistake widows make is not to understand and accept that their lives will be changed.

---

ought to prepare as well as we can for widowhood. How? Even now, after having been through it, I have no pat advice. For each of us the experience will be different, since each of us is a different individual. But I do believe there is something in the scheme of life that makes man and woman, together, complete and that death of a husband leaves a woman peculiarly broken.

I am sure that one way to make this less severe is for a woman to remain all her life a person, not just a wife. To have some interests of her own (this will enrich her family, even though indirectly). This takes thinking about yourself as an individual. It means cultivating a sort of aloneness now . . . each of us is alone in the end.

I think a young woman should start preparing for widowhood when she gets married! This may sound morbid but it isn't. The way you build your marriage from the beginning will determine whether or not you remain a person in your own right and retain a certain amount of independence. It is important to be able to make decisions and go ahead on your own even though married.

Much of this is a mental attitude. Some women, for instance, give up driving a car when they acquire a husband. This is a symptom of dependence—a small one, but a symptom—of a woman's giving up her individuality. And I suspect it's sometimes brought on by laziness rather than by a mistaken concept of being a dutiful wife!

Still a woman can be self-sufficient in many things yet crumple vulnerably when she's left alone. I certainly found this out. But there must be the resolve to carry on. The struggle is worth it for your own sake, as well as for those around you.

I am quite sure, for instance, that husbands, who love us, will help us if we are willing matter-of-factly to look at the possibility, and to plan ahead. Certainly the business side should be talked about and thoroughly planned for. Since this involves money, we've come to face the need for wills, insurance, joint bank accounts, and understanding the family business.

For when a woman loses her husband, to have to make important decisions about business matters is just the last straw. You couldn't care less just when you need to care most. Since this is woman's nature, any good husband and loving wife should have worked out all necessary plans "in case something happens." This is not being morbid—just practical.

"Till death do us part"? No. For me my husband's spirit lives in the fields he tended, the trees he planted—in our

children and grandchildren and in our faith that we are
not left alone.

—*Ruth Buxton Sayre*
as told to Gertrude Dieken

ROOTS

"You plant them early in July," she told me,
The son who didn't know the pleasures of the old days.
"Come February, the frost will take out all the bitterness—
Fixed right, they make the first good eating of the year."

So I planted parsnips and planned, come February,
To take them to her to fix right, for who else could?
We'd eat them together, relishing old-fashioned ways
That meant nothing except to our kind.

But February did not come for her, just November
With a cruel coldness that was not the weather only,
That was the weather least of all.
The greentops of the parsnips fell and died—their time.

A pile of leaves now rests within my garden,
Beneath which parsnips roots lie snug against the cold.
I stand and stare today, too long, at that low mound.
It looks like Mamma's grave.

A last and tenuous link between her soul and mine,
Between old days dying and new ones yet to live,
Between an old woman saying good-bye
And a young man, taking root.

But who will cook those parsnips, come February,
Who will eat them, relishing rich old ways?
And will the frost, by then,
Take out the bitterness?

Gene Logsdon

*T*o ease distress of the spirit, nothing equals bread making. I made bread today.

This morning started early. Bonnie, our eldest, was going away to college—she'd be our first to leave home. Her father was driving her and it would be a long trip. He called her at 4:30: "Bonnie Jo! Let's go!"

As I turned on lamps to cheer the early bleakness, I asked for breakfast preferences. "Eggs," Bonnie said. "Two for me," she added with determined heartiness.

Judy, 15, came downstairs wearing curler gear, which made her look wired for space. I launched into light ban-

---

Each step in breadmaking was a satisfying parallel to my mother role.

---

ter—"What's progress at Cape Canaveral?"—and Judy laughed. But Bonnie was quiet. Dad was quiet, too, and solemn. His "Bacon for me, Mom" came out gruff.

Bonnie left her breakfast unfinished and went up to her room. I followed. Janie, who is eight, was still in bed. "I'll miss you, Sis!" she sang out sweetly. "I'll miss you, too." Bonnie answered.

Dad yelled up the stairs for a pillow. "I might want to rest on the way," he explained, and I quipped, "Will you stop the car first?" Judy laughed. She was laughing too much. I was working too hard at being funny. Bonnie was far too quiet.

Bonnie opened the door to young Jimmy's room. "Bye, honey," she whispered. Jimmy awoke, startled. He said, "Oh." Then, "G'bye." I was rummaging in his dresser for Jimmy's little New Testament. "Do you mind if Bonnie takes it?" I asked. But he was asleep again.

I handed the Testament to Bonnie. "He won't mind," I said. She accepted it awkwardly. This was an unreal moment, a part of the whole unreal morning.

"Let's go!" Dad shouted.

Out by the car I told Bonnie, "Now you be a good girl."

"I will, you'll see."

"Hah!" said Judy.

As the station wagon pulled away, the yard light showed me Bonnie's valiantly waving hand. Daylight crept across the sky like a thin yellow cat.

On that September morning, while my loneliness wept inside me, I made up a big bowl of yeast dough. I lived with that dough through its lifetime. In its early stages I kept it warm like it was a baby. I watched it grow; and when it got too big for the bowl, I disciplined it by punching it back to size. When it gained the satin of its first maturity, I molded it with my hands, then placed it in suitable pans and awaited developments.

Each step in my bread making was a poignant, satisfying parallel to my mother role. Bonnie would have been astonished to know I was bringing her up all over again!

The bread was out of the oven by mid-afternoon. It was now golden and finished, and did not need me anymore.

There will be other partings, as our other children go forth from home. But the first aching wrench has been faced and dealt with—gently assuaged by a timeless and creative bit of homecraft.

—*Joyce Ferris Swan*

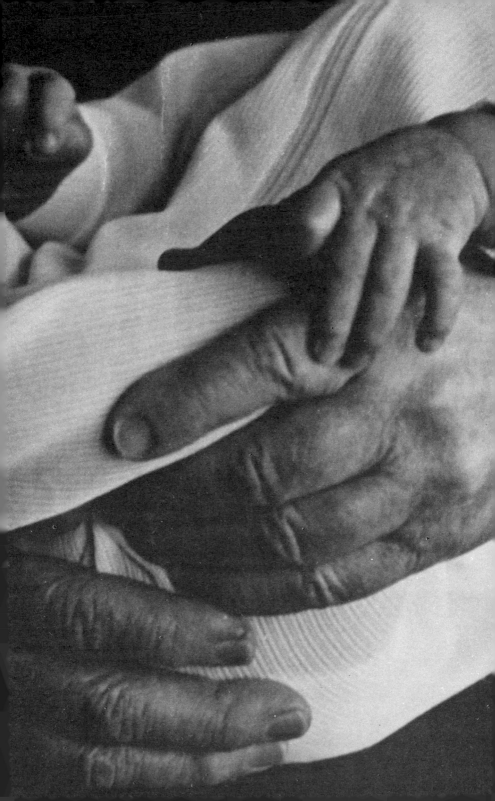

The Rewarding Years
ETERNITY

Martha

When she was young—stories danced through
   her brain
Beating their wings and crying to get out.
"Wait!" she would say, "tonight when the last
   dish is dried
I will write you."
But when night came—her tired body drifting
   off to sleep murmured "Perhaps tomorrow."
So years passed.
And there were her stories, broken incoherent
   things,
"Write us down now," they pleaded, "before
   we are gone forever."
But always she answered "Tomorrow I may
   have time."
They were in the pies baked in the oven,
   the corn thrown to the chickens,
They were scrubbed into the rough pine boards
   of the farm house

And darned into countless socks, the wind
    fluttering the wash on the line knew them,
    the bees in their honey-gathering heard
    her whispering them to herself.
But always—"Tomorrow I may find time to
    write them down."
Then she was old—
Tired hands folded in her tired lap;
Tired eyes dully watching the spring's promise.
Not in a story's pages her talent,
But in three stalwart sons, who would pattern
    life to come
After her, whose scripture was selflessness.

—*Blanche Bostock*

$\mathcal{G}$eorgie died last night. Georgie was our cat. A plain, old, everyday cat. But to my 4-year-old son, Jerry, Georgie was the first experience in friendship outside our circle of family love. Georgie brought him mice; he gave Georgie cookies. While my son shrank back in fear, Georgie fought the raccoon, who in Jerry's eyes had come to eat the kittens. Georgie and Jerry had shared emotions—had, in a 4-year-old boy's world, ridden the river together.

And now my son had found his cat lying dead inside the barn door. He came to me with dread stamped on his face.

Even as he cried, Jerry began to ask questions and he asked all the right ones.

He had seen death, but did not know what death was.

"Daddy, Daddy. Georgie." That is all he could say. Afraid to say more perhaps, afraid that his words would make it come true.

I found the shovel and slid it under Georgie and lifted her. And right then Jerry knew death for sure, because Georgie would never have allowed herself to be picked up on the end of any shovel on earth.

Tears streaked down his chin, but I had nerve for only one look into eyes that were second by second learning about the world that ends all living with dying.

I turned my back, walked resolutely toward the woods, my shovel heavy beyond all rational explanation. And he came along, though every whimper and wail protested.

Even as he cried, Jerry began to ask questions and he asked all the right ones, all the unanswered pleas of all men in the face of death. But I had to answer.

"Can she see us yet, Daddy? Does she know she's on that *shovel?*"

I did not say what I wanted to say. I did not tell him that Georgie was up in some cat heaven, smiling down on us from a misty world where the mice were thick and plump and the milk heavy with honey.

"No, Jerry, Georgie can't see us anymore."

"Can't she even feel? Can't she move at all?"

"No, she can't move or feel at all."

"Make her move." Jerry grabbed me around my leg, begged me, the man who, in his eyes, could do anything in the world.

"I can't, Jerry. When something is dead, you can't do anything about it." I laid the shovel down, and held his head against me and knew I wasn't going to be able to take it much longer.

"We must bury Georgie," I finally said and started on again toward the woods.

"What is bury?"

"We will dig a hole and put Georgie in it and cover her up," I explained.

"Why?"

We were almost to the woods and I did not really know why we had to cover Georgie up with dirt.

"That is what you do when something dies."

"Can I touch her, Daddy? Does she feel the same as she did before?"

"You can touch her if you want," I said, and the boy stooped and petted his dead cat. He was the scientist now, moving swiftly from the fear of primitive man to the dawn of scientific curiosity. He was trying to diagnose death, and I could not endure it.

"We will put Georgie in the ground so nothing will disturb her," I said.

"Will you put a fence around so nobody can step on

her?" Jerry asked. I think I know how cemeteries got started.

"Put a rock on top so nothing can get her out," he said. I couldn't believe my ears. He didn't know about tombstones but his mind was surely the mind of all mankind.

"Yes, that's a good idea. Go by the barn there and get one of those rocks to put on top." It gave him something to do while I shoveled in the dirt.

But the hole was not wide enough and he was back with the rock before I got the crude rites of burial over with. Then as I started to push the dirt in, Jerry began to cry again, and I had no more strength left in me. We wept together. I wondered why, in an odd sort of way, I could weep now over so insignificant a cause—harder even than when my mother died—but my arm was around my son, and perhaps I wept for him. Or perhaps because I did not have to push the dirt on Mother's grave.

"Won't she ever, ever, ever get back up?" Jerry bawled, begging for immortality—the poor, bleating cry of all men, in all times. And I could only shake my head.

"If the old cats didn't die, there would be no room for the young ones. If our old hens didn't die, where would we keep the pullets?"

I don't know whether he understood, or even whether I did, but that is what I said because I didn't know what else to say, and we filled in the dirt and went away. Wiser? Perhaps. Jerry knew something more about death; I knew something more about mankind.

But that was not quite the end of it. Jerry appeared to dismiss Georgie from consciousness. But he spent much more time with his kitten, Georgie's last gift to him.

For three days, his kitten wouldn't eat, and my wife and I worried. If the kitten died . . . was it too much to ask of a boy four going on five? We spent a lot of time trying to make the kitten eat, with a cheery airiness, as if to show Jerry that there was nothing more normal than a kitten that didn't eat for three days. We didn't know that the boy was not fooled.

Then on the fourth day, I was up at the barn with the chickens and I heard a whoop of pure joy. Jerry was running up the path to me, his kitten in his arm.

"Daddy, Daddy, Frisky *ate* his food. He's going to be all right now. He's going to *live!*" And the bright boy-eyes shone up at me with all the hope that has kept man going for who knows how many millions of years. And I think Jerry has learned more than he realizes he has learned. Now he sees that Georgie is dead, but Frisky lives. Someday, I will die, but *his* son will live. And then he will understand how I feel now: Mother is gone, but Jerry lives, *and so then does she.*

—Gene Logsdon

ACROSS THE YEARS

Ah, lost sweet summer, windy hills and hollows,
Wide lonesome fields where flaming hawkweeds grew;
Clear skies of June laced with the flight of swallows;
Ah, shadowy hay-sweet barn that once he knew;
House by an orchard where the harvest apples
Ripened and tumbled in the sunny grass:
I must go back and back to where the dapples
Of sun and shadow flicker as they pass
Across the window sills. House, do your floors
Laugh with the dancing feet of children now?
Barn, do the swallows nest above your doors?
Is hay piled fragrant in your dusty mow?
I must go back across the years and find
The dream of peace that lingers in my mind.
                                    Leona Ames Hill

254

*O*n the long, lazy afternoons of my childhood, Grandmother used to tie on a big white starched apron, get out her basket of quilt scraps and head for the apple orchard. It was nice and quiet there, she said, in the shade of those old lopsided trees. But if she wanted solitude she seldom got it, for one or more of us grandchildren usually trailed along. There might be such a thing as a peppermint hiding in the bottom of her basket!

Our minister said Joe had entered eternity. But Grandmother said nobody can enter eternity.

Grandmother would find a comfortable spot to sit, probably on the shady side of the Maiden Blush tree, and soon the click of needle against thimble would blend in with other busy sounds: insects droning; in the spring, the clucking and cheeping of mother hens and chicks.

If autumn was coming on, an apple might fall with a soft plop in the grass; if a child didn't pounce on it, wasps and bees would swarm to tunnel in for sweetness.

The orchard fell away gently toward the pasture where we could see our cows lying placid in the shade of the river trees. Then came the fields, rising toward the hills that folded into each other—higher and higher, blue deepening to indigo and then purple.

It was not a setting where one's thoughts would often take a dolorous turn; yet it was there in our orchard that I learned from Grandmother about death—and eternity.

Because of what she told me, I often return mentally to the orchard.

As a 6-year-old I did a lot of wondering. I had noticed that the people in our community seldom used the word *died*. They skirted this deftly, for instance saying that Joe Billings had "passed away." Our minister said Joe had entered Eternity, but my grandmother took issue with that. "Nobody can *enter* Eternity," she said with conviction.

Now, polishing one of our russet apples on my dress, I asked: "Grandma, what's wrong with saying Mr. Billings entered Eternity?"

She took off her glasses and wiped them thoughtfully. "Eternity began a long time ago. No one can say for sure how long; but for a starting point let's say it began on the first page of Genesis. You know about that, don't you?" I nodded, reciting: "In the beginning, God created the heaven and the earth."

"That's right," my grandmother said. "Heaven and earth, and all of time. That's Eternity."

She sewed a couple more patches together. Then— "Look," she said, pointing. "There's the barn lot up there. Here, next to it, is the orchard; and there, over the fence, are the pastures and fields and hills. Let's say the barn lot is that part of Eternity which was here before you were even born. This orchard is the part where you are now. The pasture and fields, and those high, mysterious-looking mountains—let's say they're the part of Eternity you'll learn about when you leave the orchard. It's all connected, see?"

I thought this over. "But Grandma, that means we're in Eternity now!"

"Exactly!" How pleased she was at my logic. I got a peppermint for it.

Grandmother was not the first to reflect that eternity is here and now. But she was the one who first told *me* about its immediateness and its endlessness. Now that I am grown, and sometimes aware of my years, the picture she gave me—of eternal change and progress—brings me serenity. Why count the passing of my days in one place any more than in another? I feel so sure that life is all of a whole, a forever continuing chain.

The moment a weak, human thought creeps in, like "Half my life is gone already," or when I hear someone say, "Poor Jones, his days are numbered," my memory comes to the rescue. It takes me back to our orchard and lets me see again the meadows and fields sweeping up to those far, mysterious hills.

—*Jean Bell Mosley*

*I*n a few weeks—or maybe a few days—I shall die. I shall leave my husband, my two teen-age girls and my blue-eyed Richard, who is only 12. Every relentless tick of the clock measures off what remains of my life. *Yet I am a happy woman!*

If anyone had told me, even a year ago, that the verdict "incurable cancer" would leave a trace of happiness for me, I would not have believed it. Because of this . . . and because death comes to every family . . . I am writing my experiences of these last days, when my life is in sharp focus. For *I am one of the lucky ones* who is granted the opportunity to prepare for death.

My philosophy and faith didn't develop the minute the diagnosis hit me. This is how it was:

A year ago last September, like any wife and mother, I was busy trying to "serve my turn" for each of my three children. I jumped hurdles to make committee meetings, to bake 12 dozen cookies for the YWCA fall cookie sale, to serve Sunday night supper to 30 of Jackie's Senior High Youth Fellowship group.

All this was in full swing when I came down with what we thought was flu. Like any mother, I stayed on my feet to help with a boy-girl Camp Fire party, so important to my teen-agers. But by that time I knew I didn't have flu. Hepatitis, we thought.

After several months, the doctors recommended exploratory surgery and I had it. When I asked what they had found, the surgeon said "induration of the pancreas." I didn't look it up.

I took him in my arms and explained what I had learned in the hospital . . . . There were tears and we mingled them.

A couple of weeks later the surgeon's bill came to the house, and I opened it. That was the first I knew that I had cancer. It said so, plainly, on the bill: Carcinoma.

Carcinoma! No, not in my family! The closest it had ever struck was my grandmother's sister. It couldn't be.

The pancreas is one organ on which a biopsy needle is seldom used; the diagnosis couldn't be definite. So for a year we lived under a cloud of cancer that might not prove a certainty.

What a wonderful year it was, nevertheless. Maybe because my husband and I knew there was a chance I wouldn't be around, life became more precious. As I look back now, I see that we crowded some extras into space and time—things we might otherwise have postponed.

We went on family vacations—a week in Minnesota, near Lutsen; two glorious weeks of camping, hiking and fishing in the Grand Tetons. A family dream—having a farm near Ames—came true. And we bought a riding horse, which, plus the one we could borrow, meant that we could ride in pairs.

This was our year of preparation, I'm sure. Even though we didn't talk about the possibility of my illness recurring, deep down my philosophy was forming. And deep down my faith was being bolstered with the kind of miraculous strength that comes from outside ourselves when we need it.

We came back from our vacation to another typical fall. The campus and children's schedules soon were in full swing. I met myself going and coming, probably with an inner determination to keep everything normal. One day I diced potatoes for a church supper; next day went to a Master Farm Homemakers' luncheon; next day helped our tenant's wife give a turkey dinner for the five families that had helped them move.

I can see now that my mind and heart were extra watchful. I would catch a special meaning in a sentence in a speech—one that probably would have escaped me before. Like the statement, at a women's meeting, that a homemaker's efforts should be measured in the happiness moments that she gives her family. Something impelled me to slip away from this particular meeting, skipping the dessert, so that I could join my husband who was going out to the farm.

I was living in high gear—but then I always had. I would rather live 42 full, rich years than twice that long in dull tempo.

The pace ended abruptly last fall. I went back to the hospital for surgery, which I knew would tell the truth.

After surgery, I asked no questions. But my private

nurse and friend whispered, "I wish there were some magic word I could say ..."

There was no magic. There was no medical cure. This I knew. All right, my lot was no different from the thousands of others who die of cancer every year. Right then and there I accepted the inevitable. I ruled out bitterness and resentment. None of this "Why should it be I?" Why *shouldn't* it? Cancer kills indiscriminately. My background of science made this a logical fact to accept. The logic doesn't erase the great inner loneliness of every soul faced with departing from life. But this "giving up the controls" is the first big step.

The hardest part about accepting death philosophically was the awareness that I was walking out on three teen-

---

Instead of going to the city for recreation, we've taught our children to love the outdoors.

---

agers and my husband. At what seemed to me a time when a mother's counsel was a daily need. I must confess tears dampened my pillow when I wrestled with that one.

Then my wonderful young minister came with a book for me—*A Diary of Private Prayer* by John Baillie. God must have guided me quickly to these words, for they were the answer to my concern for my family:

I am content to leave all my dear ones to Thy care, believing that Thy love for them is greater than my own.

I asked my minister to mark passages in my Bible that would be particularly helpful in preparing me for death. These are the passages he marked and these I have concentrated on: John 14:1-3, 18-20; 16:16-23, 25, 33; and all of chapters 20 and 21. Romans 8:35-39; I Corinthians 15:35-

260

44, 54-58; II Corinthians 5:1; Philippians 1:20-23; I Thessa-
lonians 5:1-11; Revelations 21:1-4.

The next big step was to rule out steadfastly all wish
thoughts for the future. Family plans, personal projects ... all my dreams I just forgot about. For I knew that
my happiness and serenity (and therefore my family's)
would rest on the fact that I simply live for each day.

The day before Christmas I came home from the hospital. For ten weeks now, I have looked death in the eye,
and I can truthfully say that each day has been gay, filled
with peace of mind, and overflowing with thankfulness
for the wonderful and thoughtful things that friends and
family do.

Why, I would be less than grateful if I complained or
were bitter or unhappy. Just as I had all the breaks for
real happiness during my 42 years of living, so am I still
having all the breaks! How different if I were lying
racked with pain and saw my family struggling to take
care of me and the house. Cortisone has relieved nausea;
other new drugs have relieved much of the pain. A wonderful housekeeper has come in to relieve me and leave
me free to enjoy my family and friends. And I am so
grateful for this period that lets us visit about the children and their needs. (She will stay with my family when
I am gone.)

I am determined to keep these last weeks as normal as
possible for my family. Why, when I have spent years
creating a happy home for them, should I give up now
during these last weeks when they need the assurance of
normalcy more than at any other time in their lives?

The children know, of course. We told them. I told Alice
and Richard, the two youngest. My husband always has
been closer to our oldest daughter, Jackie, so he told her.

Alice, being 13, simply said she didn't believe it. She
mentioned one of our friends who had been thought to be
incurably ill, but who survived. So Alice has come to the

realization gradually, which is good.

Richard, 12, is my baby—I took him in my arms and explained to him what I had learned in the hospital and that I would be leaving the world. There were tears—and we mingled them. I tried to explain that it was God's will.

My husband—well, we had our year of preparation. His jolt came at the very first—before I had seen the hospital bill with its news—and he lost 20 pounds during those weeks when he was alone with the knowledge. It was not easy to philosophize with him when at first he brooded in so-human fashion: "Why did it have to be you?"

There is a temptation, when Time is running out, to crowd advice and admonitions into the last moments.

Something impelled me to slip away, skipping dessert, so that I could join my husband.

That temptation I will not yield to. In the first place, I think death-bed advice and "promises" can be horrible things—promises sometimes even exacted for selfish peace of mind of the departing. Circumstances can change decisions and situations.

And I am not unmindful of the truth that the drama of death may impress my influence on my children's lives so that it may be greater than if I were to remain routinely with them! God works in mysterious ways.

Through the years I've repeated and repeated some of my pet philosophies and I'm sure they're now a part of the children's code of living if they're ever going to be. I've said it a hundred times in various ways: "I'd rather see you flunk than cheat."

Another thing we have impressed on the children: "It's

easier for you to learn to play than to work, so we'll teach you to work." Instead of joining the country club, we substituted gardening and Saturday afternoon farm work. I don't know how much character we've built into our children by having them chop bull thistles, paint farm buildings, or hold pigs for vaccination, but at least these have been family projects.

We've tried to keep their feet on the ground in other ways, too. Instead of going to cities for recreation, we've taught our children to love the outdoors. "Some day you might lose all your money and all your friends," we've predicted philosophically, "but if you can enjoy the outdoors you can still enjoy life." We've hiked, we've picnicked, we've gardened, we've been bird-watchers, we've hunted and fished.

I feel that all these things remembered in the years ahead will speak louder than any words I could say now. We have worked for years to establish the pattern.

It takes a tight grip on my emotions, now and then, I'll admit. Our daughter Jackie is a senior and we have been discussing college. That is what we would normally be doing this time of year. I catch my breath when Jackie, talking calmly about her future, intersperses a remark like . . . "unless I get married." My mind tells me the thing to do is to respond lightly, "Oh, we're getting married?" when my heart wants to take her in my arms and cry, because I will not be around for this milestone in my daughter's life.

But for me, Time begins with each new sunrise. I have not taken to my bed—why should I husband my waning strength? Life has been good—there is no urgency to prolong it.

In these past few weeks our home has been "open house" with a full pot of coffee and a sampling of food brought in by friends. These visits have made my days glow with happiness.

When friends drop in, it's their experiences I want to

hear. By listening, my own life stretches out and I no longer feel bound by space or time.

Mrs. Raymond Sayre, my 50-miles-distant neighbor (formerly president of the Associated Country Women of the World), came by, for instance. As she showed me a basket of treasures she had picked up in her recent Middle East travels, I found I had the time and compassion to consider the very real problems of the Arab and Jew.

One friend comes in every week and shampoos and sets my hair; a registered nurse stops in to give me a back rub. Another friend helped my daughter cut out a dress for a box social . . . important to a teener. A friend who plays the piano beautifully drops in to give me music. On Sunday, my friend's voice teacher is coming to sing "The Lord's Prayer," a favorite of mine.

I have the time to savor this daily richness. The hyacinth someone has grown specially for me smells twice as fragrant as one bought at a greenhouse which I might have smelled so carelessly before.

I have no regrets—my life has been rich and full, and I have loved every minute of it. But if I were to live it over, I would take more time for such savoring of beauty—sunrises; opening crabapple blossoms; the patina of an old brass coffee pot; the delighted surprised look on a tiny girl's face as she pets a kitty for the first time.

I would eliminate enough outside activities so that I could be always the serene core of my home—for the triumph of serenity has crystallized for me and my family in these last days. There would be more time for the family and for close personal friends.

I would get closer to people faster. When death is imminent we open our hearts quickly and wide. How much more Christian love there would be if we didn't wait for death to release our reserves!

I would live each day as if it were my last one, as I am doing now.

— *Hazel Beck Andre*

I don't know how many times we told her not to climb up in the haymow to throw down bales to her calves. But Mother wouldn't listen. She never listened to people telling her to take it easy. People had been telling her all her life not to carry heavy buckets of feed to the chickens when she was pregnant; not to hoe her garden when her back hurt, not to get up at 4 A.M. to help with the milking when her kidney infection flared up. She paid no attention. She was contemptuous of physical weakness—and mental weakness too. She never let any of her nine children stand around

Father found her there with our dog licking her face. And she whispered that Tillie licking her face felt good.

feeling sorry for himself. "When you grow up and get yourself some real problems, you'll think you deserve the luxury of a nervous breakdown," she would tell us. And then she'd give us more work to do.

So there she went, all alone, up into that mow again, probably singing (she was always singing), and at 57 she could climb a barn ladder as spryly as a 17-year-old. But something happened this time. No one will ever know how, but somewhere along the edge of the mow, she lost her balance and fell. Fell and broke her neck. Broke her neck and died.

But it didn't happen all that fast. She was too tough to die that easily. She lay in the manure, unable to move or cry out. Father found her there with our dog licking her face. She whispered that Tillie licking her face felt good.

Even now, three years later, I can barely force myself to think of it. I don't know how Father could take it. I was not there, but I cannot take the thought of it. I want to hold my father in my arms and love away that memory. But he stood it. And my brother stood it. And my seven sisters stood it. Because Mother had taught us that you can stand anything when you have to.

In the hospital, the doctors put a pin in her head and attached a weight to it so her neck would not move. She complained only that they took away her false teeth which none of us children knew she had worn for twenty years. Her head had to be shaved, and ugly as that seemed to make her, for the first time I could tell how very much she looked like her father.

He had never given up either. When he was 84, he demolished his pickup truck and walked away unhurt. After that the family would not let him drive from his house in town to the farm. So he walked. By the time he was 90, he'd become confused, walk the wrong way and get lost. They forbade him to leave the house. So he'd sneak out. Finally they took his shoes away from him. That was the only way they could keep him off his land.

And I remembered Ed Hesse, the old Minnesota farmer for whom I had worked as a hired man. When he lay dying, shot through with cancer and a couple other diseases, no one of which was enough to kill him, to the very end he kept sliding his good leg out from under the covers and banging it against the bed rail. "See," he'd say. "I still got one part of me in good shape."

And so now, my mother. She lay in the hospital a week, refusing to give up. She was paralyzed from the waist down, but wouldn't admit it.

"Look, Gene," she'd say. "See how I can move my hands. See how strong my grip is." And I'd have to put my finger into the palm of her hand and she would try to grasp it. She could not turn her head to see that her hand, which had held nine children growing up, which had gripped countless hoe handles and tractor steering wheels and horses' reins, which had pulled milk from who knows how many cows, could not now hold on to even my slack finger.

But she kept working at it, flexing her arms, all day, all night. We could tell when she was conscious that way. Her hands would quiver, clench, open, clench. Even when she had no strength to talk, the fingers kept up the fight.

Finally she announced to all of us that she had given herself a goal. By the time Rosy, my sister, had her baby

---

My sudden, unbidden laugh rang out over the quiet cemetery. My children, who were with me, did not understand.

---

in the spring, she'd be able to sit in a wheelchair and hold it in her arms, she declared. That's what she told us. And kept repeating. It was the very last thing she said to me.

But that is not the end of the story. Old farmers, like old soldiers, never die. They stamp a piece of land with an indomitable spirit that lives forever. This is how I know.

There were long gray days after that burial, days not fond to recall, when about the only thing that kept us going were those words of hers which had kept us going before: "When you get yourself some real problems, you'll think you deserve the luxury of a nervous breakdown." I was traveling extensively, as usual. Always before, I could lift the telephone in Chicago or New York or wherever, and call home and she would always be there. So now I tried again to call down those long, lonesome wires of the homeless. But no one would answer. Father was there, but he was always someplace working. Sisters were there, but they were always out. No one would answer. And that is how I finally came to accept that Mother was dead. She was not home anymore.

A day came when I could go back to the cemetery. It was early spring in the flat Ohio country, with only a little greening to it. I walked to the grave, prepared to have the sorrow all plowed up again. I was thinking about how stupid cemeteries were, the irrational symbolism of granite and flowers and live people standing over bones becoming earth again. And maybe that feeling of irrationality prepared me for what I found on Mother's grave, because what I found bears not the scrutiny of logic.

What did I find? A bird, a killdeer, sitting on a nest of eggs, on top of Mother's grave. The bird fluttered away at my approach, screaming in defense of her brood, pretending that she was hurt, luring the intruder away from the life it was her duty to protect.

Mother always loved killdeers—she liked to call our farm Killdeer Place. I had to smile. Ignoring the tombstone, I stooped to examine the eggs. Infuriated, the killdeer charged me. She held off, an arm's length away, seeming to stamp her foot in the very way Mother used to do when she was angry. My sudden, unbidden laugh rang out over the quiet cemetery. My children, who were with me, did not understand. My children saw a bird and three eggs in the grass. I saw the spirit of my mother, screaming in defense of creation, turning even her grave into a green cradle of life.

—*Gene Logsdon*

Index to Authors

Titles listed are those under which articles and poems originally appeared in FARM JOURNAL.